RENEWING THE COUNTRYSIDE

Iowa

RENEWING THE COUNTRYSIDE

Iowa

Editors:
Shellie Orngard and Jan Joannides

Senior Photographer:
Jerry DeWitt

Art Direction and Design:
Brett Olson

Published in Partnership with the
Leopold Center for Sustainable Agriculture
the
Iowa Natural Heritage Foundation
the
Iowa Rural Development Council
and the
Institute for Agriculture and Trade Policy

by
Renewing the Countryside

Renewing the Countryside — Iowa

Editors Shellie Orngard, Jan Joannides

Senior Photographer Jerry DeWitt

Art Direction Brett Olson

Writers
Michael Mayerfeld Bell
Michael Carey
Charles Carpenter
Jim Cooper
Karol Crosbie
Shelly Gradwell
Amy Hassinger
Mary Swalla Holmes
Nate Hoogeveen
Jerry Johnson
Paul W. Johnson
Willy Klein
Heather Lilienthal
Molly McGovern
Laura J. Miller
Peter Nessen
Denise O'Brien
Shellie Orngard
David Osterberg
Diane Ruth Phillips
Leigh Rigby-Adcock
Jim Rudisill
John A. Schillinger
Bill Silag
Larry A. Stone
Mary Swander
Mike Whye
David L. Williams
Bill Witt

Printer Sigler Printing and Publishing, Inc., Ames Iowa, USA

Paper 80 lb. Reincarnation Matte
100% recycled, 50% post consumer waste
New Leaf Paper, San Francisco

Sponsors We greatly appreciate the generous financial support provided by:
- Leopold Center for Sustainable Agriculture
- Iowa Natural Heritage Foundation
- Practical Farmers of Iowa
- Humane Society of the United States
- Center for Respect of Life and Environment
- Institute for Agriculture and Trade Policy
- Northern Great Plains, Inc.
- The Northwest Area Foundation
- Great Plains Institute for Sustainable Development
- United States Department of Agriculture—Cooperative State Research, Education & Extension Service

ISBN 0-9713391-2-0 (hardcover); ISBN 0-9713391-3-9 (paperback)

Library of Congress Control Number: 2003095652

Address inquiries to Renewing the Countryside
2105 First Avenue S, Minneapolis, MN 55404
1-866-378-0587 · rtc@iatp.org · www.renewingthecountryside.org

First Printing

*We dedicate this book
to the individuals and
families working each day
to renew Iowa's countryside.*

FOREWORD

Iowa's heritage lies in its rural and farming communities. *Renewing the Countryside* is a collection of stories that recognizes our history and will awaken readers—rural and urban alike—to the wealth of creativity that is producing successful ventures in the rural and farming communities of Iowa.

These stories demonstrate the lives and livelihoods of people who are taking advantage of their natural surroundings to produce quality products and services, creating a sustainable, prosperous future for our great state. This book is a showcase for some of the most unique and appealing elements of Iowa's rural areas and small towns.

From the time I first came to Iowa, I have been impressed by the strength and beauty of our rural communities. The people of rural Iowa have a genuine love for their communities, and an incredible spirit of generosity, hospitality, and civic participation. Here in Iowa, we are working to transform our rural economy to become rooted in the production of high-value agricultural products. We have unprecedented opportunities to harness the wind to produce clean, renewable energy, to convert the crops we grow into clean, renewable fuel, and to spark a new generation of entrepreneurialism that brings the health of the environment into the economic equation. Iowans throughout the state are working to build a transformed economy that will boost our local economies, provide incomes that will support families, and generate the resources to sustain the values that are at the heart of our quality of life.

I hope you will enjoy learning more about Iowa's countryside—and the great people that are leading its renewal.

Thomas J. Vilsack
Governor, State of Iowa

TABLE OF CONTENTS

FOREWORD — 7

INTRODUCTION — 11

CONSERVATION - CHAPTER ONE — 13

Bringing back the tall grass prairie—*Carl Kurtz and the Prairie Creek Wildlife Refuge* — 14

A family's gift to future generations—*The Connell family and Lone Tree Point Nature Area* — 17

Turning marginal cropland into profitable pastures—*The Petty family's Iowa River Ranch* — 20

Working together for healthy, productive woodlands—*Prairie's Edge Sustainable Woods Cooperative* — 23

Saving heirloom plant varieties from extinction—*Seed Savers Exchange* — 26

An Iowa farm, from the abstract to reality—*Essay by Paul W. Johnson* — 30

FARMING - CHAPTER TWO — 33

Sun-ripened hogs—*The Willis Farm and Niman Ranch* — 34

People of the land: Establishing new roots—*Maichoa and Blong Lee* — 37

Your neighbor or your neighbor's farm?—*Dick Thompson and Practical Farmers of Iowa* — 40

Raising boys, growing vegetables, spinning wool—*Janette Ryan-Busch and Fae Ridge Farm* — 43

Farming in partnership with nature—*Essay by David L. Williams* — 46

ARTS, TOURISM & CULTURE - CHAPTER THREE — 49

An illuminating business—*Bogenrief Studios* — 50

Biking where the trains once ran—*Wabash Trace Nature Trail* — 53

Van Buren rising—*The historic villages of Van Buren County* — 57

From horseback riding to stargazing—*Garst Farm Resorts* — 59

Building on a community's heritage—*Manning Hausbarn* — 62

The value of staying put—*Essay by Michael Carey* — 64

MARKETING - CHAPTER FOUR — 67

Marketing vegetables Cleverley—*Cleverley Farms* — 68

Incubating stay-at-home businesses—*Franklin County Cottage Industries* — 71

Milk with a reputation—*Radiance Dairy* — 74

Relationship marketing in southwest Iowa—*Audubon County Family Farms* — 77

Come meet the people who grow your food—*Des Moines Downtown Farmers Market* — 79

Marketing as conversation—*Essay by Mary Swalla Holmes* — 82

PRODUCT INNOVATIONS - CHAPTER FIVE 85
    Iowa's goat cheese pioneers—*Northern Prairie Chevre, LLC* 86
    The aesthetics of tofu—*Wildwood Harvest Foods* 89
    Unsour grapes—*Iowa's emerging wine industry* 92
    Envisioning a new agrarian landscape—*Southeast Iowa Nut Growers Association* ... 95
    Iowa ingenuity at work—*Essay by John A. Schillinger* 98

ENERGY - CHAPTER SIX 101
    Harvesting the wind—*Waverly Light and Power and Spirit Lake School District* ... 102
    Farmers fueling energy independence—*West Central Cooperative* 105
    Fields of energy—*Chariton Valley Biomass Project* 108
    A better place to work—*Iowa Association of Municipal Utilities* ... 111
    Energy policy transforming the countryside—*Essay by David Osterberg* ... 114

COMMUNITY - CHAPTER SEVEN 117
    Building a community food system—*University of Northern Iowa Local Food Project* ... 118
    Working together for a bright future—*Park View Inn & Suites and Conference Center* ... 120
    Locally grown food delivered to your door—*Sunflower Fields CSA* ... 123
    Rallying around habitat restoration—*Ida County communities committed to conservation* ... 126
    Tomatillos among the soybeans—*Diversity Gardens in Lenox* 128
    That glorious song of old—*Essay by Mary Swander* 130

LEARNING - CHAPTER EIGHT 133
    Slow Food in Iowa City—*Chef Kurt Friese and Devotay* 134
    Hooking people on land use issues—*LaVon Griffieon and 1000 Friends of Iowa* ... 136
    Empowering entrepreneurs—*Penny Brown Huber and Growing Your Small Market Farm* ... 139
    Cultivating a spiritual connection to the earth—*Prairiewoods Franciscan Spirituality Center* ... 142
    Some things you can't learn in a classroom—*Iowa State University's Life in Iowa program* ... 145
    Changing the face of agriculture—*Denise O'Brien and the Women, Food & Agriculture Network* ... 148
    Learning to renew the spirit, the farm, and the community—*Essay by Charles Carpenter* ... 150

AFTERWORD 152
ACKNOWLEDGMENTS 154
PUBLISHING PARTNERS 155
PHOTO AND WRITING CREDITS 156
STORY CONTACT INFORMATION 158

INTRODUCTION

TWENTY-SEVEN years ago when I decided to leave a career in higher education in the Boston area to return to a small rural community in North Dakota to take over the management of our family's farm, both my colleagues at the university and my neighbors in North Dakota were incredulous. Why would anyone deliberately choose to go from success to failure, they wondered. Rural communities, especially agriculturally dependent rural communities, have been seen as failed communities for some time, both by those who live in them and by those who view them from afar. Over ten years ago Margaret Udansky, in a front page story in *USA Today,* declared that small rural towns had outlived their usefulness —that they had "a lot of history, little else."

This book of stories about real people, living in real rural communities, bears witness to the fact that Udansky was dead wrong. The failure of rural communities is not inevitable. Rural communities, in fact, are showing signs of renewal. And rural communities are still great places to live.

These are stories about people living in their own little corners of rural Iowa who have quietly begun a transformation. They are "renewing the countryside." Through their imagination, dedication, and entrepreneurship they are each bringing new hope to the rural landscape—a landscape that many have written off as being beyond hope.

The purpose of this book is three-fold. It is intended, first and foremost, to acknowledge the people of Iowa who in their own quiet way are renewing the countryside in their own communities. We could only include a few of the many great stories of rural renewal in this volume. We trust that the stories featured will serve as a source of inspiration to young and old alike and that they will encourage Iowa's youth to consider pursuing their own dreams in Iowa's rural communities.

Secondly, we hope that these stories will motivate rural and urban citizens to recognize the rich resources that exist in Iowa's rural communities and that they will support those communities by buying locally and investing in local businesses. To help the reader more readily obtain products and services from the families featured in this book, an appendix provides information to help the reader contact these entrepreneurs. We also hope that these stories will inspire all of Iowa's citizens to become more actively engaged in their communities to develop rules and regulations that are friendly to local entrepreneurship and local investment.

Thirdly, we hope this volume will encourage policymakers and government servants to take a second look at our rural communities. Rural communities have been a rich resource for the nation since the earliest settlements—from First Nations people to the present day. These stories tell us that, given the opportunity, our rural communities can still be vibrant centers of business and culture—communities that can serve our nation well for centuries to come.

We hope that you enjoy these stories as much as we all have enjoyed collecting them and bringing them to you. And please join us in our efforts to continue renewing Iowa's countryside.

Frederick Kirschenmann, Director
Leopold Center for Sustainable Agriculture

CHAPTER ONE
Conservation

Conservation is a concept most people understand and can embrace. Whether it's protecting wildlife habitat or cleaning up a river, we all believe in protecting our natural places—at least to some degree.

The pioneer generations and their immediate successors, who worked tirelessly to clear the tall grass prairie for conventional row-crop production, did not foresee the impacts of the demise of that unique ecosystem. Today, by contrast, government agencies, nonprofit organizations, and private landowners seem to share an appreciation for what once was and a desire to see it reestablished wherever feasible.

The problems often come when conservation goals come into conflict with economic goals. In this chapter, we learn of people who have found ways to bring profits into conservation or who have been willing to make personal sacrifices for a greater good. It is dedicated people like these who prevail on behalf of all of us, and on behalf of future generations.

BRINGING BACK THE TALL GRASS PRAIRIE
Carl Kurtz and the Prairie Creek Wildlife Refuge

Tucked on a hillside in north central Marshall County lies the farm of Carl and Linda Kurtz. On a mid-October afternoon, harvest season is in full swing. On the Kurtz farm, however, the scene is unique. While neighbors whiz through hundred-acre fields of corn and soybeans with thirty-foot-wide combines, Carl and Linda use a small 1969 John Deere self-propelled combine to wade through a breath-taking mix of grasses and flowers swaying in the autumn breeze. For over twenty-five years, Carl has been working to bring back the tall grass prairie on his farm, otherwise known as the Prairie Creek Wildlife Refuge. Amidst the fragrant seed-heads, buzzing insects, and flitting birds, one captures a glimpse of what our ancestors may have seen when they first came to Iowa.

The diverse plant communities of the tall grass prairie once covered more than 90 percent of Iowa's original landscape. Most of Iowa's native prairie is now under intensive cultivation. The less than 2 percent that remains is mostly found in small parcels in varying states of degradation. Through his planting and harvesting methods, Carl Kurtz is expanding what remains of Iowa's original tall grass prairie. The harvest occurring on the Kurtz farm is much more than prairie seed. Clean water, renewed soil, biological diversity, and a stunning example of a viable farming enterprise are among the benefits.

Carl Kurtz is a modern day pioneer. His talents are as diverse and complementary as the plants in his prairies. Carl is a long-time naturalist, professional photographer, conservation leader, sustainable farmer, author, musician, lay minister for his rural church, educator, and one of Iowa's leading experts in prairie reconstruction.

Carl has lived most of his life on this farm bought by his father in the 1930s. His parents instilled an interest in the wild parts of the farm and encouraged him to take the time to explore them. "I liked to go hunting. And I used to hunt almost every day after school, year 'round. That was a way to be connected, to be out there," says Carl.

This early cultivation led Carl to a degree in Fisheries and Wildlife Biology at Iowa State University. He also gained an interest in photography during college and while serving in the Army. He developed his photography skills while using them as a tool to observe and capture changes in the landscape. "You can really see changes in things if you keep photographing them as they go along," explains Carl. Photography originally drew Carl to prairies. Upon returning to his farm after the Army, he met botanist Roger Landers and joined him on research trips around Iowa to learn about and photograph unique natural areas. "That opened up a whole world to me," explains Carl. "He was a good ecologist, and he introduced me to prairie vegetation."

In the mid-1970s, Carl began to see that current agricultural practices were contributing to degradation of the soil and water. In response, he began implementing sustainable agriculture practices on his farm, such as strip-cropping and contour farming. This led to soil losses far below the average. Carl began witnessing and documenting the improvements in his farm's health and was increasingly guided by his interest in the ecology of the land.

The history of prairie plantings on the Kurtz Farm had humble beginnings. In 1975, Carl scattered some prairie seeds in an attempt to vegetate the poor soils

of an adjacent roadside. A year later, motivated by his desire to photograph prairie and its wildlife, he converted three acres of cornfield adjacent to the homestead. Over the next twelve years, Carl would reconstruct an additional thirty-five acres of cropland and pasture using seed purchased from dealers.

This time marked the beginning of a marriage between Carl's diverse passions: photography, wildlife, farming, prairie, and sustainability.

As the prairie developed, Carl made many observations about its effects on the land. There was now a stunning display of wildflowers throughout the growing season. An abundance of pheasants, deer, grassland birds, butterflies, and frogs provided inspiring subjects for photography. Carl believes that "the charm of the prairie lies in what it attracts."

Carl also noticed more practical benefits of the prairie, including the return of the soil's capacity to hold water and filter nitrates, even in large rain events. This was evidenced by the remarkable purity of the farm's wetlands. Carl says, "I began to realize that natural systems do not deplete themselves or the land. Soils become richer and more productive as the diversity of plants and animals that utilize them increases."

In his careful observations, Carl also saw the flaws in his plantings. The areas with fewer flower and grass species had a greater weed infestation. "A grassland is just fine, but it's not very stable," he explains. Carl concluded that plantings lacking plant diversity were not as dynamic and declined over time. In addition, he noticed, that a diverse system catered to a greater diversity of wildlife. This theory that "there is stability in diversity" became the cornerstone of Carl's prairie philosophy.

Carl started to focus on what he witnessed as the single barrier to planting a large number of species—the very structure of the prairie seed industry. Up until this time, prairie seed had been grown in large monoculture stands and sold as individual species. And as Carl observes, "You can't believe the problems inherent in that system, including weed, insect, and fungal pressure." The maintenance and harvest of monoculture seed plots is extremely labor intensive. Those costs are passed on to the consumer. "What I saw about this whole business was that if you really wanted to get a planting that had a lot of diversity, you couldn't afford to do it," Carl says. "I thought there must be a better way to raise the seed, to get diversity, and get the price down."

In 1990 the opportunity arose for Carl to manage and harvest a twenty-acre remnant of beautiful, diverse, original Iowa prairie in nearby Story County. Using his seemingly endless ingenuity, Carl converted his old Allis Chalmers pull-type combine into a prairie harvesting machine. He took the harvested seed and planted the first acres of what would become the Kurtz's prairie production plot. Since that time, Carl has converted a total of fifty acres of his farm using this precious, native seed. These plantings have matured into stable prairie reconstructions, which Carl now harvests in bulk each fall. He sells the resulting product to landowners wishing to restore a dynamic prairie system.

"Our goal is to get people to plant big plantings, but you've got to get the cost down so they can actually do that," remarks Carl. In developing this revolutionary way of harvesting and marketing prairie seed, Carl was able to reduce the cost of a diverse planting by 75 percent. "That gave us a market that, in a sense, nobody had."

One of the most striking features of the operation is the Kurtz's economic success. Today, the Kurtz farm is composed of 60 acres of production prairie, 120 acres of other prairie reconstructions, and 90 acres of corn and soybeans.

"The prairie has enabled us to have a very small farming acreage operation and make it," says Carl. "That's a big deal. We're making enough money to not only support us, but to go out and purchase more land. It's a very small, sustainable system."

Carl's method has numerous benefits for his customers. When purchasing the seed, central Iowa customers can be sure they are getting seed native to this area and, therefore, best adapted to grow here. They know they are getting a mix containing fifty to sixty plant species. The result will be a dynamic, stable prairie planting that improves over time. With the seed comes Carl's caring advisement and his more than twenty-five years of prairie establishment experience. "Good things come out of caring about people and trying to help them however you can within the limits of your time. Part of the success of it is persistence and hanging in there with people," states Carl.

In the last twelve years, one might say Carl's prairie seed and planting methods have spread like wildfire. Carl has worked with over one hundred individuals and conservation agencies to plant well over one thousand acres of prairie in central Iowa. He has pioneered steps for establishing a successful prairie. His extensive use of mowing in prairie establishment has since become a standard practice. Carl shares his expertise in his book *A Practical Guide to Prairie Reconstruction*. Countless other seed dealers have also adapted Carl's approach to planting, harvesting, and selling prairie seed. Many of his Marshall County neighbors have used his seed in their own plantings, exponentially increasing the benefit to local wildlife. Hundreds of individuals come to see the Kurtz farm every year.

Carl is humble, yet hopeful about the broader influence of his work. "I think the impacts of things like this are like any other sustainable operation. They are really subtle. It just grows a little bit. You touch a person here and you touch one there. And then they go out and do the same thing. Those kinds of things actually last. It's like planting a seed. You just plant them here and there and everywhere and you see what happens."

A FAMILY'S GIFT TO FUTURE GENERATIONS

The Connell Family and Lone Tree Point Nature Area

Shoreline paths and walking trails through the oak grove forest beckon to the visitor. Come in, they bid; embrace nature. The trails are part of an Iowa gem of natural heritage—Woodford-Ashland Lone Tree Point Nature Area—on Clear Lake's southwest shore.

Jan Lovell grew up taking walks there with her "Gramp," Earl Ashland. She remembers helping him plant walnut trees. She learned to respect and care for this special place from him and her parents, Jim and Marcia Connell. Connell family memories and an appreciation for nature have been built around hiking through wildflowers, hunting mushrooms, enjoying family picnics, and days spent exploring at Lone Tree Point.

"This is a very special place of peace and quiet," says Marcia Connell. "It has been a special, almost sacred place to many, many people for a long time. It's good for the soul here." She continues, "My father knew every detail of this land. Our love for this area brings us close to an oasis of wilderness and close to each other. My parents worried about how to protect this area, how to keep it in its natural state."

For over one hundred years, Marcia's ancestors made nature preservation a family value, keeping the Lone Tree Point area just as it had been when settlers came to the area in the 1850s. The 101-acre area includes 4,600 feet of natural shoreline, 84 acres of timberland, and 11 acres of wetland. Besides morel mushrooms, spring wildflowers, and other flora, the area is home to native wildlife including red fox, wild turkeys, Canadian geese, and ducks.

Preserving the area in its natural state was a concern that Marcia inherited with the property when her mother passed away. It was worrisome, until ten years ago. In 1992, the family found peace of mind when Marcia and Jim Connell and their three daughters and sons-in-law donated a conservation easement on the property to the nonprofit Iowa Natural Heritage Foundation (INHF), guaranteeing protection of the area.

"We wanted to retain ownership of the property and make sure that it would never be developed," Marcia explains. "The Iowa Natural Heritage Foundation was an organization that would work with us as owners to preserve the area."

By placing a perpetual conservation easement on the property in 1972, Marcia and Jim Connell and their daughters and spouses—Jan and Tom Lovell of Clear Lake, Sarah and Dennis Ohlrogge of Onalaska, Wisconsin, and Susan Connell-Magee and Kevin Magee of Madison, Wisconsin—ensured that the property was protected from development beyond their lifetimes.

The conservation easement removed development rights from the property, so current and future owners are not entitled to develop this land. The conser-

vation easement further restricts other uses that would be detrimental to the land's natural features, and it gives INHF the authority to monitor and enforce the easement in perpetuity. Now the family can look forward to passing the land into new hands, knowing that its natural features are protected.

"Conservation easements are a growing thing in Iowa," says INHF's vice president, Anita O'Gara. "We are seeing easements on all kinds of property for a variety of reasons. Some are set up for water quality issues, others for wildlife habitat or scenic purposes. Each one is unique."

Anita explains that Woodford-Ashland Lone Tree Point Nature Area's uniqueness is twofold. It is a natural shoreline on a natural lake, and it offers public access, which is not typical of other INHF private land conservation easements.

When landowners, like the Connells, begin thinking about a conservation easement they need to ask themselves whom their conservation partners will be. Who will they ask to protect their property into the future? This

conservation partner could be the county conservation board, the Iowa Department of Natural Resources or other approved public agencies, or a nonprofit group like INHF.

Other questions that need to be answered include issues of ownership of the land, future restrictions on the land, desire for compensation, and the importance of tax advantages. The Connell family answered these questions. Their answers and a family legacy of commitment to preserve the area's natural state led them to establishing the Woodford-Ashland Lone Tree Point Nature Area and the permanent conservation easement.

The area's easement allows for limited public use for hiking, picnicking, and cross-country skiing. It calls for gentle use—no vehicles or horses, no camping or fires. Access to the area is made most easily by boat. Visitors can enter by foot on the east edge of Ventura Heights.

"Many people visit the area, but the land has not been changed by people," says Jan. "What we are seeing is a natural return of wildflowers, the return of native flora and fauna to areas that were in cow pasture twenty-five years ago. Trail maintenance with the help of volunteers, friends, and the Iowa Natural Heritage Foundation is the only visible human impact here over the last ten years."

Looking to the near future, Jan says the family is exploring ways of enhancing the natural process to return some of the area to native prairie. They are also planning to restore a 190-acre adjoining working farm into wetland and prairie to complement Lone Tree Point Nature Area.

During the last decade, INHF has had the responsibility to regularly monitor compliance with the terms of the conservation easement. This is done by regular inspection visits arranged with the Connell family. The foundation's staff walks the land, documents its condition, and prepares a monitoring report. They also answer management questions and provide technical assistance and names of experienced land managers in the area who can assist with management issues.

In this time of state and federal budget cuts, conservation easements are a cost-effective way to retain some pristine areas. Easements throughout Iowa are a tool that keeps open space permanently in a community. Even when they don't allow public access, such easements offer scenic and wildlife benefits, often water quality benefits, and help retain an open, more rural character wherever they are located.

Ron Andrews, Department of Natural Resources wildlife specialist in Clear Lake, explains that there is a significant, positive environmental impact in Lone Tree Point's natural shoreline. "This conservation easement protects the shoreline and the vegetation which attracts more wildlife to the area," says Ron. "Protection like this typically increases the diversity and density of wildlife in the area. There is potential for heron rookeries should heron decide to establish here. There is also potential for eagle nests as that population increases and this area is protected. But that will be up to nature, not man, to decide."

Woodford-Ashland Lone Tree Point Nature Area benefits the Clear Lake area in several other ways. The area acts as a natural filter for water entering the lake and because it will never be developed, it will never add urban pollution to the lake. And the area is openly used as a recreation and tourist area by the public and provides public access to the lake.

"It also provides green space—a place to reconnect with nature," says Jan. "I believe that is basic to our human needs—to feel connected to the natural world around us. Preserving this opportunity for future generations—that's what this is all about."

TURNING MARGINAL CROPLAND INTO PROFITABLE PASTURES

The Petty Family's Iowa River Ranch

Dave Petty has made a career of taking marginal cropland and overgrazed pastures and turning them into profit on his Iowa River Ranch. Good business and good stewardship go hand-in-hand for this Hardin County beef producer.

Along the eastern bank of the picturesque Iowa River, the Petty's cow/calf, cattle-feeding, and crop operation stretches for seven miles between Eldora and Union and spans nearly three thousand acres. About half of the land is rented from twenty neighbors; Petty and his wife, Diane, own the rest. Dave and three employees tend thirteen hundred acres of soybeans and corn (most corn is fed as supplemental rations to cattle), with the rest of the land in pasture and hay. In addition to the cow/calf and cattle-feeding operations, they finish about one thousand hogs each year for market.

Conservation practices abound on the Petty's family farm—and so do the wildlife, including deer, ducks, and pheasants. The first three miles of the farm is native timber, which the Petty family has preserved for hiking, horseback riding, family camping, canoeing, and fishing. Then the land opens up to rolling hills, wooded ravines, and river bottomland, perfect for grazing the Petty's five-hundred-head Angus herd. By renting from neighbors and buying land as it has become available, Dave has pieced together twenty-two paddocks, all connected with their own source of water.

The system Dave has established allows cattle to be moved from one area to another, grazing in pastures or in fields of leftover cornstalks nearly ten months of the year. By rotational grazing, Dave keeps the grass at its maximum vegetative or growing height of about four inches. Shorter grass can become overgrazed and taller grass goes to seed and loses its nutritive value. "You get two free things in this business—sunlight and rain," explains Dave. "If you let the grass get too tall, you waste all that sun and rain." Dave moves his animals about every week, depending on the weather and the age of the cattle. Each pasture might be grazed three times during the year.

Although he grew up in nearby Union, Dave's parents quit farming when he was in high school. In 1974, he began working for an area farmer after attending Hawkeye Community College in Waterloo. That same year he struck out on his own, buying ten cows and renting pasture from a neighbor.

"I began renting small pastures when no one else wanted to do that," Dave explains. "Commodity prices were high and everyone wanted to raise corn and soybeans. Much of this land along the river was rough ground and not suited to farming."

Each time he added a new property, he made improvements. He cleaned out scrub brush. He reshaped waterways, improved drainage, and built holding ponds protected by uphill terraces. Dave reseeded pastures and turned marginal crop fields into forage. He interplanted with high-quality red clover and birdsfoot trefoil when the ground was still covered with frost so that growth could begin with the spring thaw.

"We've tried to respect the land and treat it as our own," Dave says. "I really think neighboring farmers watched what I did with other people's property, and then they would rent their marginal land to me too."

Some improvements have been extensive. In one pasture, Dave drilled a new well, laid four thousand feet of underground water line, and plans to add another two thousand feet. When completed, the system will provide six watering areas for cattle.

"When I started, this pasture had a washout large enough to park a semitrailer truck in it," he says, pointing to a field which now has only gentle curves. Even in early August the field is bright green with new clover. "The cattle probably think they're in heaven to have fresh clover this time of year," he remarks.

Dave estimates that in cooperation of the Natural Resource Conservation Service, he has built thirteen miles of terraces on the crop ground, installed twelve miles of drainage, reshaped more than eleven miles of waterways and seeded three miles of buffer strips.

Dave uses conservation in other ways too. He uses minimum tillage, practices contour farming, and applies manure from his feedlot operation as fertilizer for corn crops. He also plants grass in headland areas around cornfields, which is baled once during the season to keep the grass growing. By the time the corn crop is harvested, the grass provides other nutrients to cattle that graze cornstalks.

These efforts helped Dave win the National Cattlemen's Beef Association Region III Environmental Stewardship Award, and then be named the national winner among seven regions. Also in 2002, Dave received the

Environmental Protection Agency's Regional Administrator's Award for Environmental Excellence, the first given to a farmer.

Dave has been active in the Iowa Cattlemen's Association, serving two times as its president. During those terms he helped lead a new producer cooperative that sought to operate its own slaughter plant in Iowa. With nearly a thousand producers on board, Dave is confident their work will someday capture a market in Japan.

"The key is to keep an operation small enough so that farmers can still make their own management decisions," explains Dave. He is proud that he has built his operation on good relationships with his neighbors and did not take over anyone else's business. "I built it on my own, and that's why I have a burning desire to keep it together," he says.

"Farming also needs to be fun," says Dave, which is why the Pettys have added a primitive campground near the river in a portion of native timber. The land often becomes a weekend gathering spot for picnics, hikes, trail rides, canoeing, hayrides, campfires, and fishing expeditions for their extended family that includes sixteen nieces and nephews under age eight.

Almost every evening in the fall, Dave walks a half-mile trail from his house to the river just to enjoy the place. "There was a time when you used to have fun in agriculture, but people seem to have forgotten about that," Dave says. "We've tried to add some fun into our operation."

WORKING TOGETHER FOR HEALTHY, PRODUCTIVE WOODLANDS

Prairie's Edge Sustainable Woods Cooperative

Healthy profits from healthy forests: "We can have both," according to northeast Iowa landowners who have formed the Prairie's Edge Sustainable Woods Cooperative. It's an old concept with a new twist. Individuals pool their ideas and assets to pursue a group venture that might overwhelm one person.

Several tree farmers launched the cooperative idea in 2001, after becoming frustrated with the complexities of marketing timber from small tracts of land. They also hoped to promote woodland protection and restoration. In two years, the coop grew to seventy-seven members with more than eight thousand acres of woodlands. The enthusiasm for the coop, even with a one-hundred-dollar membership fee, showed the strong commitment of many landowners to sustainable forestry.

Prospective members cited a host of expectations for the group, which was patterned after similar cooperatives in Minnesota, Wisconsin, and Michigan. A brainstorming process resulted in more than one hundred suggestions for the Iowa coop including: a store or website to sell unique forest products, woodland tours, certification of wood that is grown sustainably, a code of ethics for loggers, pooled bids for tree planting and harvesting services, woodworking classes, and landowner education workshops.

To test these ideas, the coop commissioned a feasibility and marketing study by the Community Forestry Resource Center of Minneapolis. A fifteen-thousand-dollar Sustainable Agriculture Research and Education grant from the U.S. Department of Agriculture paid for the study, a promotional brochure, and four issues of a coop newsletter.

Despite the favorable response to the concept, however, Prairie's Edge members were sobered by the disbanding of the Sustainable Woods Cooperative of Spring Green, Wisconsin, in 2003. That cooperative had embarked on an ambitious wood processing and marketing operation, but apparently incurred too much debt and was forced to close.

With a Rural Enterprise Business Grant through the Northeast Iowa Resource Conservation and Development office, Prairie's Edge prepared a business plan to see if a northeast Iowa coop might fare any better. The study acknowledged the difficulty of joint marketing, manufacturing, or sales of wood products—but noted the potential of the cooperative to provide education and land management services. Accordingly, Prairie's Edge has set its sights more on services to members.

A draft action plan proposed modest steps to get the coop on a firm footing, while providing services to satisfy old members and attract new ones. For example, the coop might contract for timber stand improvement (TSI) work, tree planting, marking trees for harvest, horse logging, custom sawing, or timber appraisals. A marketing consultant, paid by a Rural Development Through Forestry grant from the Iowa Department of Natural Resources, surveyed forestry professionals to learn what services they could provide. Coop members would pay for the forestry work, with a portion of their fee going to the coop for administration.

Prairie's Edge also has conducted or plans to hold workshops on how to do a timber inventory, tree seed collecting, forest wildlife management, winter tree and shrub identification, chain saw safety, raising shiitake mushrooms, and other forestry topics.

A next goal for the cooperative, which has been organized and run by volunteers, is to hire a part-time coordinator—perhaps using money remaining from the grant to prepare the business plan. The coordinator would arrange forestry services for members, plan educational programs, and schedule inventories of members' woodlots. Those inventories by trained volunteers, along with management plans for cooperative members, would help determine the demand for services.

While Prairie's Edge is still in the experimental stage, its members are determined not only to improve their woodlands, but also to make the cooperative a success. For example, board member Ron Berns of Monona has gradually acquired 210 acres of timberland over the past thirty years, and he manages another seventy acres with two other partners. One of his motivations is to prevent the land from being developed. That's also a concern of other woodland owners who've seen the growing demand for wooded acreages for home sites and for hunting or other recreation.

Ron regularly works in his woods, cutting ironwood trees to provide nurse logs for a shiitake mushroom grower, harvesting mature or damaged trees to sell to a sawmill, and selecting lower grade trees for use in construction projects around his farm.

Board president Kevin Sand is a family practice doctor in Decorah. He's been planting trees since his college days, and now owns several timber tracts, including woodlots that have been in his family for many years. Vice-president Phil Specht of McGregor, one of the founders of the coop, is a dairy farmer with a longtime interest in woodland conservation. He served several years on the Clayton County Conservation Board.

Board member Greg Koether of McGregor is a cattle producer who's learned to treat woodlands with the same respect and care as crop fields and pastures. Unlike some livestock raisers, Greg and his wife, Kathy, view woodlands as an economic asset, rather than a liability.

Garth Frable of McGregor is a planner who has used his professional skills to help organize the coop and apply for grants. His wife, Teresa McMahon, an administrator with the Iowa Department of Natural Resources, also has assisted with communications and publicity. The couple manages woodlands on the Clayton County farm where they recently built a timber frame house.

Francis Blake and his family operate an organic farm with three hundred acres of timber near Waukon. Rick Burras, a Decorah banker, manages eighty acres of timber on the farm where he lives. Mike Natvig of Cresco is an organic farmer who has used horses for logging.

Rob and Nancy Bolson of Decorah manage several woodlots on their family's farms in Winneshiek County. Rob also operates a woodworking shop in Decorah, and Nancy is a special needs teacher. Harold and Deanna Krambeer of St. Olaf own four small tracts of woodlands totaling seventy acres. They've planted and harvested hardwoods, raised Christmas trees, protected a rare algific talus slope, and simply enjoyed the woodlands' natural character.

Despite their diverse backgrounds, a strong common denominator for Prairie's Edge members is the group's motto: "Dedicated to improving the health and profitability of northeast Iowa's woodlands."

SAVING HEIRLOOM PLANT VARIETIES FROM EXTINCTION

Seed Savers Exchange

Kent and Diane Whealy were granted a sacred trust in 1971 when Diane's grandfather, Baptist John Ott, gave them seeds of two varieties of garden plants—a tomato and a morning glory—which his parents brought with them when they emigrated from Bavaria to the United States in the 1870s. Grandpa Ott died that winter, and the Whealys realized the two rare varieties would vanish if they did not grow the plants and harvest and save the seed.

How many more varieties of vegetables, fruits, grains, and flowers were on the verge of extinction, they wondered. Because most gardeners buy seeds from the limited, mostly hybrid varieties offered in the catalogs of major suppliers, many thousands of standard varieties were in danger of becoming extinct. Kent and Diane regarded these disappearing varieties as "heirlooms," important both for their historic and scientific value.

In 1975, the Whealys founded Seed Savers Exchange (SSE), a nonprofit organization dedicated to the preservation and distribution of heirloom varieties. The mission of SSE, based at Heritage Farm near Decorah, Iowa, is clear and simple. "We want to increase the genetic diversity that's available to farmers and gardeners," Kent says. "We have found that there is a tremendous heritage of heirloom garden plants in this country that was brought in by the original immigrants. Gardeners and farmers always brought the best of their seeds with them. We want to preserve those links."

Kent explains the importance of heirloom seed preservation, both for the science of plant genetics and the record of America's history and heritage. Plants that have evolved in different regions of the world have different genetic characteristics, alterations in their genetic makeup that might enable them to withstand stresses—such as drought, insect pests, or plant diseases—or allow them to thrive in harsh conditions or poor soils. Plant breeders can use these genetic characteristics to develop varieties that can grow and produce food in dry seasons, marginal soils, or summers beset by high populations of damaging insects and diseases.

In a world of hybrid varieties of garden vegetables based on a limited range of genetic stock, the potential for widespread crop failures is increased. And the genetic material needed to develop hardier varieties is diminishing. The lesson for plant breeders is clear: when you tinker with the engine, do NOT throw away any of the parts—you may need them later.

Equally important is the history and heritage of America's gardening and farming culture. The heirloom seeds offered by Seed Savers Exchange include varieties of garden plants that are intertwined with the great events and people of our past.

"We have seeds in our collection that supposedly came over on the Mayflower," Kent says, "and there are varieties of tomatoes that General Robert E. Lee sent home to his family during the Civil War."

The Seed Savers gardens grow flowers, herbs, and vegetables that Thomas Jefferson raised in his gardens at Monticello and beans and corn carried by members of the Cherokee Tribe on the Trail of Tears. "Every family has its own seeds and every seed has its own story," says Kent. "That cultural heritage is really incredible."

Seed Savers Exchange has more than eight thousand members around the world and coordinates the distribution of some twenty thousand varieties of heirloom garden seeds. About three hundred of the heirloom varieties it offers are available in bulk quantities, a valuable resource for community supported agriculture (CSA) operations, specialty growers, and alternative seed companies.

SSE grows, harvests, stores, catalogs, and distributes heirloom varieties grown at Heritage Farm and in the gardens of SSE members around the world. In addition to the varieties that immigrant gardeners and farmers brought to North America, SSE preserves traditional varieties grown by Native American, Mennonite, and Amish families. For more than twenty-five years, SSE has been a leader in the heirloom seed movement, and its members have distributed an estimated one million samples of endangered seeds not otherwise available.

The annually published *Seed Savers Yearbook* is the world's greatest single source of heirloom varieties. It contains listings of more than twelve thousand rare varieties of vegetables and fruits and the addresses of the eight hundred SSE members who offer those seeds for distribution.

Heritage Farm, SSE's nine-hundred-acre headquarters and demonstration farm, is a living museum of historic varieties and maintains more than twenty-four thousand rare vegetable and flower varieties. Its classic barn was restored by Amish carpenters and features a cathedral-like roof arching over a huge hayloft that serves as a meeting area and performance hall. The barn also contains a visitor center and garden workshops. Up the hill, an oak post-and-beam building contains SSE's modern seed storage facilities and a complex of offices and meeting rooms.

Heritage Farm is open to the public for tours, and it offers educational programs for school children and other groups. The most popular tour opportunities are walks through the Preservation Gardens and the Historic Orchard.

The Preservation Gardens are open from Memorial Day until October, 9 a.m. to 5 p.m. daily. Visitors can walk through these beautifully landscaped, certified-organic gardens where some two thousand endangered varieties are grown for seed each year. They can tour the Historic Orchard, the most diverse public orchard in the world, where more than seven hundred varieties of nineteenth-century apples and two hundred varieties of hardy grapes are maintained and displayed. Visitors will also want to see the herd of about eighty Ancient White Park Cattle, a two-thousand-year-old breed from the British Isles that has fewer than one thousand surviving animals worldwide.

Each summer, Seed Savers Exchange hosts an annual convention on the next-to-last full weekend in July when the Preservation Gardens are at their peak. Keynote speakers have included some of the world's best-known activists and writers in agricultural and social issues, including Wendell Berry, Wes Jackson, Gary Nabhan, and Nancy Arrowsmith. About 250 SSE members take part in the educational presentations, garden and orchard tours, demonstrations and workshops, and entertainment, including a traditional barn dance.

Seed Savers Exchange uses its publications, tours, and educational programs at Heritage Farm and outreach work across the country and the world to create awareness of heirloom varieties and the efforts to conserve them. The organization has provided the models and the resources for genetic preservation projects and for the operation of seed distribution companies throughout the United States and in more than thirty other countries. It is respected worldwide for its accomplishments and continued commitment to seed conservation.

An Iowa Farm, from the Abstract to Reality

Essay by Paul W. Johnson

In 1853, a sixty-three-year-old Yankee and his twenty-eight-year-old bride built a log cabin of hand hewn oak along the Upper Iowa River and called it their home. Their farm, which is now our farm, is 150 years old this year.

I recently reread our abstract—the legal description of our farm—to get a feel for what Benjamin Culver and his wife possessed in those frontier days. I suppose I should have known that any document called an "abstract" wouldn't tell me much. My old *Webster's New International Dictionary* (1946) defines abstract like this: "1. Considered apart from any application to a particular object; 2. Used without reference to a thing or things; 3. To separate by operation of the mind."

So what did the Culvers take responsibility for in 1853? Although our abstract doesn't say it, we know that the land they homesteaded was not the same as the land we have today. The Culvers' land was home to black bears, mountain lions, wolves, bison, and elk. The river had northern pike, sturgeon, muskie, and walleyed pike in it. Millions of passenger pigeons darkened the skies over their farm during fall migration time. Today none of this wildlife calls our farm its home. Like the American Indians who also made their home on our farm, they have all been forced to go elsewhere. The passenger pigeons could find no other home, and in 1914 the last one died in a Cincinnati zoo.

Our abstract tells us that new families settled on our land in 1862, 1909 (a power company became owner that year), 1918, 1948, 1956, and 1962. Our name was added to the abstract in 1973. Eight generations of owners! But none with the same surname. Our farm's owners have been Yankees

and Irish, and offspring of Norwegians, Germans, English, Bohemians, and now Swedes. Such confusion our farm must feel!

The abstract does not tell us about the condition of the farm as each new owner took possession. But we know that by the 1930s our farm was going downhill fast. Soil erosion was so bad that the Upper Iowa River ran chocolate. Fields were getting smaller as the gullies got larger and more numerous. White-tail deer, beaver, otter, wild turkeys, and ruffed grouse disappeared. Bald eagles and red-tailed hawks no longer soared above our bluffs. Across Iowa 200,000 farm abstracts were silent as land radically changed. Three million acres of marsh were drained. Twenty-eight million acres of prairie were reduced to a few hundred acres of remnants. Seven million acres of forest were cut in half. Three thousand miles of streams disappeared as we made them straight as dead snakes. By the 1930s, fifteen billion tons of rich, black Iowa topsoil had been carelessly squandered. Our abstracts recorded no loss.

Fortunately, efforts have been made over the past seventy-five years to halt further degradation of our land. Conservation districts were formed in every county, and federal and state governments provided technical and financial assistance for private landowners through the Soil Conservation Service, now the Natural Resources Conservation Service.

Although we have much yet to learn and do, the most onerous abuse of natural resources on many of our farms has now lessened. Our rivers are burdened with less sediment as we gain greater understanding of the need for soil conservation. Deer are back in our fields—in fact, there are now too many deer! Otter and beaver swim again in our streams, and once more we hear turkeys gobbling across our valley on frosty spring mornings. Eagles and hawks soar and screech overhead, and at night the coyotes yelp in a loud chorus. Can the wolves be far behind?

We've now been on our farm for thirty years. During that time we've milked cows, raised sheep, chickens, and beef cows, grown and harvested corn, soybeans, oats, hay, Christmas trees, gardens, and launched three more Johnsons into the world. With the help of our children and the inspiration of our grandchildren, we are farming our land with deepening understanding and respect. Like many of our neighbors, we're restoring prairie and experimenting with soil-building crops and pasture rotations. We now delay harvesting the centers of our hayfields until the bobolinks have fledged each June. Wild flowers and young trees are coming back in our woods since we fenced out the livestock. A new local forestry co-op has formed to promote more sustainable woodlot management. And we hear stirrings of a new effort to remove the old dams along the Upper Iowa River so it can once again run free. Maybe someday our grandchildren will catch pike in the river in front of their two-hundred-year-old farmhouse.

We still sleep every night in the Culvers' 150-year-old log cabin. We do so with reverence. But even more importantly we sleep each night knowing that our farm is on the mend. No longer do we feel the urge to completely domesticate the land as we farmers have been driven to do for the last thirteen thousand years. There is room on our farm for other life—life that is wild—as well as the cultivated plants and animals that give our fellow humans their food and fiber. Many Iowans share this new vision of agriculture and what it means to be stewards of land. Perhaps someday, maybe 150 years from now, our abstracts will become real and will record

what we really possess when we own a farm. Let's hope, for the sake of future generations and for the sake of the farms they will inherit, that those abstracts will record a rich abundance of life and the cultures that have been supported by that life.

Paul Johnson is a former director of the Iowa Department of Natural Resources and chief of the Natural Resources Conservation Service. He also served three terms in the Iowa House of Representatives and is co-author of the 1987 Iowa Groundwater Protection Act.

CHAPTER TWO
Farming

In Iowa, the word "farming" typically stirs up images of vast fields of corn and soybeans. But other farming happens in Iowa, as you will see in this chapter. These stories are about smaller scale enterprises that show a concern for balancing human demands on resources with the earth's capacity to sustain life.

Read about a farmer raising hogs in a manner that respects the animals and the environment. And about new Iowans who have found a way to build on their deep cultural traditions of farming. Learn about a group of farmers who have embraced research to help them farm in ways both profitable and neighborly. And learn about a hard-working woman of the earth who has raised everything from vegetables to boys to bunnies.

The farmers portrayed here are innovators whose visions of a new Iowa countryside extend beyond production agriculture to the social and spiritual dimensions of life in Iowa for generations to come. For them, a life in agriculture is the pursuit of a dream—to provide for one's family, yes, but also to leave the land, the water, and the entire ecosystem that has sustained them in better shape than they found it.

SUN-RIPENED HOGS
The Willis Farm and Niman Ranch

Paul Willis likes comparing hogs to tomatoes. Given the choice, which would you rather eat: a fragrant, vine-ripened tomato, or a tasteless, perfectly formed hothouse facsimile? A taste comparison of a pork chop from one of Paul's hogs with one from a hog raised in concrete confinement prompts him to dub the latter "hothouse hogs."

Fewer than ten years ago, Paul—as well as most like-minded farmers—was struggling to make a profit from his farm-raised hogs. "We were raising the best pigs and being paid the worst price," he says. Today, the "best" pigs are rapidly gaining popularity, and farmers are receiving significant bonuses for raising them.

Paul's practices are hardly revolutionary. "We raise pigs the way they used to be raised in the state," he explains. A visitor to Willis's seven-hundred-acre farm comes away with an understanding of the old-fashioned term "hog heaven". These pigs are happy. Here, approximately one thousand hogs are kept in seven different locations. A pickup ride through one of the hog pastures (which soon will be rotated to grow crops) is instructive and pleasant. Piglets race through the grass, and birds swoop overhead. A half dozen young pigs curiously approach the pickup. Odor is minimal.

Paul frowns and jumps out of the truck. "These guys need to be sorted," he says, noting an older pig that is out-of-place with his younger piglet comrades. He pulls a larger pig away from a suckling sow to make room for the smaller feeders. "We know our animals are raised for food, but in a way, they're almost like pets. They deserve a certain level of respect. They should be allowed to be pigs."

Paul's pigs do piggy sorts of things—wallowing in mud, foraging for roots, and pushing straw around to make soft beds in the small, portable huts. "If you look at their bodies, you can see what they're designed for," Paul says. "Their noses are little plows, and their tiny feet are made to walk in soft ground. They're not meant to live on concrete."

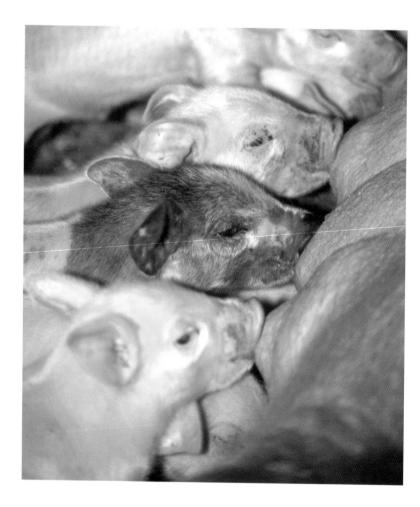

Because Paul's hogs live outdoors, and because of the particular genetics of the animals he chooses to raise, they are fatter than confinement hogs. They are also healthier—a result of more fat, more exercise, and less stress than their confinement counterparts. Willis uses neither growth hormones nor antibiotics. He doesn't need to, he says.

"If you take good care of your pigs, they aren't going to be stressed, and they aren't going to get sick. Some pigs are constantly fed antibiotics their entire lives. They've been abused environmentally and genetically to the point that this is the only way some operations can keep their animals alive."

The result of stress-free living and more fat makes a flavorful, "sun-ripened" taste, Paul explains. In contrast, confinement hogs, which are bred to be lean, can be flavorless. "It is a common practice to inject meat from hogs raised in confinement with brine after slaughter to make the meat palatable. So packing plants get a 56 percent lean carcass, inject it, and sell you a lot of water."

Regardless of the taste of the product, packing plants pay a premium for lean pork. "When it came time to sell my hogs to packing plants, I was being penalized rather than rewarded for my practices," says Paul, who is unconvinced that the consumer really wants lean pork at the expense of taste. "When people go out and order a pork chop, they're not ordering it as diet food. They're ordering it because they want something that tastes good. Consumers aren't getting their extra calories from a couple of ounces of fat from the pork they eat."

Early in 1995, Paul learned of an exciting market for his free-range pigs when he was visiting his sister in California.

Bill Niman, a California rancher and distributor of free-range meat, had made a name for himself among the chefs of the finest restaurants nationwide. These chefs have learned what Paul has known for years: animals that are treated humanely yield the most delicious meat. One taste of Paul's pork, and Bill Niman asked him to provide thirty hogs.

Paul Willis is just the sort of farmer Bill Niman's company, Niman Ranch, seeks out. Niman Ranch is committed to providing consumers with the highest quality meats and believes those meats come from farms and ranches where animals are treated humanely, fed the best natural feeds, and never given growth hormones or antibiotics.

Gourmet aficionados from coast-to-coast would agree. Niman Ranch sales top $20 million annually, and the critics pour on the praise. "One taste of Niman's pork, beef, pastrami, ham, or bacon at some of this country's top restaurants (or at your table via his online meat market) is proof that he is truly ahead of the herd," raved *Bon Appetit*, which in 2001 awarded the rancher the magazine's fourth annual American Food and Entertainment Award. "Last week is only the second time in my life I tasted pork so delicious it needed no seasoning beyond salt and pepper," wrote the food editor of the *New York Times*.

After less than four years, Paul Willis's initial supply of thirty hogs to Niman Ranch has grown to more than two thousand hogs per year, shipped on a weekly basis. Paul now contracts with more than two hundred farmers (70 percent from Iowa) and pays them a fifteen-dollar per hog premium over what they would receive in traditional markets. These farmers, like all Niman farmers, follow the humane husbandry standards developed by Diane Halverson of the Animal Welfare Institute.

Returning to yesteryear's hog-raising practices may save an industry that is coming under fire, says Paul. "In the past, the money, the manure, the hogs, and the labor were spread throughout the countryside, and it didn't really cause a problem. Hogs in concentration controlled by a few large integrators is not a sustainable system. I can't think of anything worse that could have been designed to drive people out of the state of Iowa."

There's no question that managing a diverse farm is hard work, and no question that hands-on attention to free-range animals is time consuming. But there are a growing number of Iowa farmers ready to return to sustainable practices. "I'm always looking for farmers," says Paul. "And I'm finding new, interested farmers on a regular basis."

PEOPLE OF THE LAND: ESTABLISHING NEW ROOTS

Maichoa and Blong Lee

They are people of the land, accustomed to depending on it to sustain them. But it is clear when you pass Maichoa and Blong Lee's home in inner-city Des Moines that they are struggling with their tiny allotment. The front-yard garden, even with its brave display of an American flag, speaks of meagerness.

The Lees and their relatives Yer Yang and husband Mai Vang represent two Hmong families of the approximately 169,000 Hmong in the United States, and the 280 who have settled in Iowa. In 1975, Iowa opened its doors to Laotian refugees who had been persecuted and driven from their homeland because of their cooperation with the United States's CIA during the Vietnam War.

The Lees, who lived in a refugee camp in Thailand for six years before coming to the United States in 1988, learned resiliency and self-sufficiency. Their small front yard in inner-city Des Moines quite simply was not big enough for the garden they needed. "We were shopping too much," says Blong emphatically. "Too much!"

Although Laotians are typically very private people, the Lees struck up a friendship with their neighbor, State Representative Ed Fallon. Both the Lees' and the Fallons' yards featured more fruits and vegetables than grass. When the Lees became U.S. citizens in 2001, they asked Ed to help them vote for the very first time. Then they had one other request. "They told me they needed more land," Ed remembers. "Couldn't I find it for them?"

He could, and did. He asked his friend LaVon Griffieon, a farmer and advocate of responsible land use, if she could give a few acres of land to the Hmong families to farm. "He shamed me into it," LaVon laughs. "He said, 'With 1,100 acres, surely you can find a few for them.'" In the summer of 2002, Craig and LaVon Griffieon invited four Hmong families to establish gardens on 2.5 of their acres. The federal corn base that stipulates a minimum number of corn acres prevented them from giving more, LaVon explains.

The Hmong tribes, originally a displaced people from China, settled in the rugged, isolated highlands of Laos. The Lee family shows visitors videos of their former home that reveal a culture devoid of mechanization. There is no electricity or running water; houses are made of grass and mud. Mai Vang remembers that he didn't have a pair of shoes until he was six years old.

But there was plenty of land to farm, and although the farmers walked seven miles one way to their plots and farmed with only oxen and hoes, the land sustained them. The hoe is one of the few possessions that the Lees brought with them from their old country, and Maichoa proudly shows it to guests. "We do everything with this," she says.

On the Griffieon farm, the Hmong families plant cucumbers, melons, herbs, onions, squash, spinach, zucchini, lettuce, and flowers. Some of the food is eaten, some is sold at the Downtown Farmers Market in Des Moines. Gardens are usually spoken of as "niam teb," which means "mother's land," for it is women who do the planting, weeding, watering, and harvesting. Seeds are rarely purchased, but saved from last year's harvest and traded among the families.

Videos of their home in Laos show a strikingly beautiful land—pastoral and mountainous. But there is no trace of homesickness in the families' voices. Life was hard.

There is one area, however, that Hmong families find frustrating in the United States. Children do not abide by the traditions and rules of their parents as they did in Laos. "This is the one thing where the United States is not good for me," says Yer Yang. Yer and Mai's children were all born in the refugee camp in Thailand, but Thai is not the parents' native tongue, and English is difficult for them. "My son holds his head and says 'My head is broken; I don't know anything you say.'" Yer demonstrates, holding her own head ruefully.

But despite parenting issues, Yer Yang and Mai Vang have faith in a better future for their twelve children, and the Lee's for their five children. "I believe my kids..." Blong Lee loses the English words he needs to communicate, but he raises one hand high in the air, to show a higher level of living. "They will be higher here."

The Lees' kitchen window is full of plants, which will be used to make medicine. In the living room, two baby chicks (a gift from their neighbor Ed Fallon) routinely escape from their box and run, peeping around the room. The full-grown birds are also used for medicinal purposes. Because all parts are used, grocery store chickens are not suitable.

What can Iowans learn from the Hmong farmers? LaVon's answer reflects her own passion about the importance of preserving Iowa's farm land. "We have taken an agrarian people and put them on asphalt, two blocks from the welfare office. The desire to farm burns in their gut. We do both our state and our immigrants a disservice by keeping them from the land. Will we ever embrace the diversity that we need in crops, communities, and people to sustain Iowa?"

FARMING

YOUR NEIGHBOR OR YOUR NEIGHBOR'S FARM

Dick Thompson and Practical Farmers of Iowa

Dick Thompson is standing in his machine shed, microphone in hand, striding across the front of an impromptu auditorium of folding chairs occupied by some one hundred farmers, university people, and others among the agriculturally curious. With the portable speaker slung over his shoulder Dick can move around a lot, and he does, asking for questions and answering questions, asking for answers and questioning answers: A talk-show host in blue overalls. He favors Liberty overalls, as it happens, and it says so in blue letters across the front of the bib. He is also wearing his trademark red shirt (sleeves rolled up) with black wing-tips on his feet, gold-rimmed glasses on his blue-eyed ruddy face, and a blue cap on his silver-white hair that reads "PFI: Practical Farmers of Iowa."

It's the annual PFI field day on the Thompson farm. Dick is explaining how it is that he, Sharon, their son Rex, and their daughter-in-law Lisa can make a good living for two families in an environmentally friendly way on just three hundred acres while most of the rest of Iowa's farmers are busily gobbling up their neighbors' land, and thus their communities, in order to reach the magical goal of *A Thousand Acres*—to quote the title of Jane Smiley's dark novel of Iowa agriculture. And every year a lot of people come to the Thompson farm, and to other PFI farms, to find out just how they manage it.

"Your neighbor or your neighbor's farm?" Dick repeats. "You've got to ask yourself that."

He lets the point settle in, and the crowd thinks over the seemingly inexorable advance of agricultural industrialization and modernization across the American rural landscape that each year drives out another half percent or so of farms. Most farmers in Iowa rely on their corn and soybean crops and

60 percent of the state is covered by these two plants alone, some twenty-two million out of the state's total of thirty-six million acres.

Prices vary, but in a good year a grain farmer can expect to make maybe thirty to forty dollars an acre profit—but only after the government chips in thirty to forty dollars an acre in subsidies. When the federal government is feeling particularly generous, as it has been since 1999, roughly doubling subsidies over previous levels, that figure can rise to sixty to seventy dollars an acre. Increasingly, what makes for a "good year" is not the climate in Iowa, but the climate in Washington, D.C.

Which means several things. It means that without government subsidies, the average Iowa farm, as currently managed, would be broke. It means that if you're an Iowa farmer and you want to attain a midlevel income from your farming, say $40,000 to $60,000, which are roughly the median figures for United States households with more than one person, you need something very close to Jane Smiley's thousand acres of farmland—and the industrial farming machinery and industrial farming approach that make it possible to wrest crops out of so much ground.

It also means that there will be tremendous pressure to increase your farm size by whatever means possible because Iowa currently has 33 million acres of farmland and 96,000 farms. That's 344 acres apiece, leaving the average Iowa farmer 656 acres, or almost two neighbors' farms short. In fact, something like 2,000 or 3,000 acres apiece would be better, say many, because some years you're lucky to make ten dollars an acre, even with government subsidies. That's eight neighbors' farms short—and, consequently, eight former neighbors. Under conditions like these, it's hard to pay much attention to the disappearing soil, the disappearing wildlife, and the disappearing community life that the big farm, big tractor, and big chemical way send down the creek.

However, the Thompsons get by with even less than 344 acres, and for not one but two families. By having a small farm, the Thompsons are able to manage each acre with exceptional care, minimizing reliance on the sure-fire chemistry of Monsanto and Dupont—thus minimizing cost and environmental damage as well. It's not an organic farm, but they have used pesticides only once in the past twenty years. They use no antibiotics or hormones in their pigs and cattle, they do not plant genetically engineered crop varieties, and yet they have some of the highest crop yields and lowest soil erosion rates in their county. They also have a solid, although not lavish, farm income—without government subsidies, having long ago sworn to refuse them, an act of defiance that many find particularly confounding.

Dick continues. "The problem is we're raising commodities out here, not crops. But commodities don't make communities. It takes people to make communities."

It was in 1985, during the middle of 1980s farm crisis, that a group of Iowa farmers and farm advocates found that they could no longer close their mind's eye to the decline, the abandonment, and the environmental degradation. They started Practical Farmers of Iowa, with Dick Thompson as the first president. Convinced that it must be possible to farm in economically and environmentally sound ways on small farms that support community life, PFI's founders dedicated the group to sharing information among farmers about how it could be done. They also encouraged farmers to conduct and disseminate the results of their own on-farm research.

University researchers at the time were paying next to no attention to anything other than the industrial model of farming, and very little relevant research about other approaches was available. So PFI organized field trials that would be statistically valid, using randomized and replicated plots that could be subjected to tests of significance and other statistical techniques.

The local land grant university, Iowa State, took interest in PFI's embrace of a scientific approach and agreed to form a highly unusual partnership with the organization. They gave the organization a university office and gave its few staff members (who numbered only one at the time) the status of university employees, although PFI provides the funds for their salaries. By the early 2000s, the group membership had grown to some seven hundred households, about half of which farm. And now a couple of dozen faculty and researchers at Iowa State regularly work with PFI farmers, and many of them are members of the group.

Dick says to the audience, "Some of us know what to do. The question is, will we do it?" Dick has a way of challenging his listeners that most rise to, and today's audience is no exception.

"So why won't we do it?" a middle-aged farmer in the group calls out.

Dick breaks out in a big smile. He's been waiting for this question. But he holds his own views back a bit. "Well, what do you think?" Dick returns. "What are some of the reasons?"

"Communication!" calls out one voice. "Education. It's what's in the farm magazines. Or rather what isn't in them!" calls out another.

"Ya, ya. That's part of it," Dick encourages. "But there's more to it. Keep going. Keep going."

"Cultivation, I guess," another farmer responds after a moment, meaning mechanical hoeing, one of the main ways to control weeds without chemicals. "Farmers today don't like to cultivate. It takes too long. And they don't like livestock either. That takes too much time too."

"That's part of it too," Dick affirms. "We're getting closer." He looks over the crowd in the machine shed, and the crowd looks back. The time has come to put it all together.

"Greed and ease. That's it," Dick breathes into the microphone, and a lot of heads give a slow nod of recognition and agreement at this critique of the materialist ambitions of industrial agriculture. Knowing glances are exchanged. "The other way's easier."

"But is it?" asks the farmer who had earlier pointed to the problem of what is and is not in the farm magazines. The mood in the shed is crackling now, and Dick doesn't need to ask for input. Hands are going up everywhere and a couple of people are standing. "I mean, you seem to live well. And your neighbors must see that. So what do they think? Do they ever ask you how you do it?"

Even Dick pauses at this one, and the whole shed pauses with him. "I call that a social problem," he begins. "I guess that's just the way most guys are. I hardly ever listened to my father, at least when he was alive." Dick in fact now farms quite a bit like his father, using a variant on the five-year crop rotation his father developed in the thirties and forties and hardly ever using farm chemicals. "You don't listen to those close to you, it seems. Maybe it takes a farmer in the next county doing something to show you."

Dick straightens up a bit and flashes his wide smile. He takes the portable microphone up to his mouth with both hands, and adds the kicker. "But the main issue for all of us is this: 'Do I really want to know? And if I do know, do I want to do anything about it?'"

In the case of PFI members, the answer to both questions is, thankfully, a resounding yes.

Raising Boys, Growing Vegetables, Spinning Wool

Janette Ryan-Busch and Fae Ridge Farm

On Fae Ridge Farm, just outside of Iowa City, Janette Ryan-Busch raises organic vegetables, herbs, cut flowers, goats, sheep, llamas, and angora rabbits. Geese and ducks provide insect control, and chickens help with the decomposition of garden waste. Janette is known locally as the Queen of Basil, raising ten to fifteen thousand basil plants annually. She has chosen small-scale agriculture because it is something she can manage by herself, and she enjoys the satisfaction of growing products she can use directly.

Janette grew up on a farm in southern Iowa. Her parents ran a conventional grain and livestock farm and a small grain elevator, and her grandparents raised Black Angus cattle. "Both sides of my family have been farming for generations and generations," she explains. Even though she hated picking strawberries and working in the garden, Janette's childhood instilled in her a love of the land and of hard physical work. She grew up taking care of baby lambs and calves and walking the beans. Detasseling corn, the traditional teenagers' farm chore, was out of reach for Janette—she was too short!

When her own two boys were small, Janette was determined to stay home to raise them. Already gardening to feed her family, she decided to grow and sell extra garden produce. Gardening was a way for her to be at home, be an active mom, and involve her children in something that had a community spirit to it. As Janette's boys grew, so did her enterprise. She converted a small farm building into an on-farm store. Just minutes from downtown Iowa City, customers have found a reliable source for delicious, locally grown produce and animal fibers.

With certified organic status, her loyal customer base includes neighbors, chefs, and New Pioneer Co-op in Iowa City.

Having grown up with livestock, Janette missed not having animals around, so she purchased some milking goats. While she liked the goats' energy, she found that the twice daily milking was more of a commitment than she had time for. Rather than giving up on goats altogether, she switched to Angora goats with lovely, soft fleece. After discovering that she could not make an adequate income by selling fleece right off the goat, Janette started processing the fleece. And after goats, came sheep, llamas, and angora rabbits, all of which contribute their coats to Janette's growing fiber business. "My entry into diversified small farming has been slow and constant," says Janette. "I think of it as an evolution."

Long-term planning, using yards and yards of woven fabric as a weed barrier, and incorporating a manure system are practices that make Janette's small-scale farming successful. On portions of her land, she uses a technique called sheet composting—applying manure from her farm animals on the land and then planting a green manure crop on top of that. "It is an easy way to manage manure, and the results are amazing when I plant heavy feeder crops the following year," she explains. By using crop rotation, beneficial insects, and ducks to control insects, Janette is able to keep her farm in certified organic production.

"The best times on the farm are the moments when you feel like everything is under control," says Janette. "Everything is growing and you've gotten the rain you need and things feel like they are in harmony." She loves going into the barn in the winter when it is twenty below zero outside and the barn is full of animals that are safe and warm. "I look at the animals and think, what a gorgeous flock they are!" Janette remarks that those moments are so deeply satisfying that they keep her doing what she does.

Outside of her on-farm activities, Janette has been actively involved in the organic movement. She helped start Iowans for Organic Food Standards, an organization that worked to create a labeling standard for organic production. When in 1989, the Iowa legislature passed an organic standardization law,

Janette served on the rules committee that hammered out how the organic standards law would be implemented. Her involvement took her to Washington D.C. to speak with legislators and other farm activists and to work on the national organic standards.

The state of Iowa also enacted an organic certification law that Janette helped to formulate. The bill gave the Iowa Department of Agriculture and Land Stewardship the authority to be an organic certification agency. Janette continues actively working on organic standards and certification and is pleased to participate in a project that works to help Iowans, both consumers and farmers. When she had her farm certified using this new process, she felt joyful in having helped develop a system that works and is being implemented.

Life has been interesting as a woman farmer for Janette. "Traditionally, women have been farming here forever," she remarks. "There are women in my neighborhood out driving tractors and moving cows." Janette believes that women make great farmers. They make good decisions based on compassion and a long-range perspective. While there can be some physical boundaries, Janette knows those can be overcome by being smarter than the object you are moving.

Janette believes that farming is different from other ways of making a living. One has to be flexible and able to go with the flow. "We are really connected to nature and the planet in a way that a lot of people are in denial about. Small, alternative agriculture definitely magnifies your relationship to the land."

For Janette Ryan-Busch, life is intimately enmeshed with the cycles of nature. She believes that humans must treat the earth with reverence and respect and let it call the shots. Her animals and plants are a testimony to the care that she gives to Mother Nature. She is indeed, a hard-working woman of the Earth.

Farming in Partnership with Nature

Essay by David L. Williams

I was born seventy years ago, and I have happy memories of my childhood on our family farm in southwest Iowa. In those days, we farmed with horses, growing or raising almost all of the food we needed for the entire year. We relied on the farm for most of our other needs as well. Even the fuel for cooking food and heating the house came from the timber we cut and from the corncobs we collected in the hog lot.

Doing chores by myself and with my three brothers was a daily part of life on the farm. There were meaningful tasks for the youngest and the oldest. Chores included bringing in fuel from the cob house and the woodpile, gathering eggs, feeding the chickens, helping in the garden, and forking hay down from the haymow for the cattle and horses. One of my favorite jobs was to bring the sheep and milk cows from the timber pastures into the barn lots at night. A Shetland pony and later a quarter horse helped me with that job.

As a boy, I became well acquainted with nature. In the spring I learned which were the earliest flowers to bloom and the first trees to leaf out. I learned to spot the nests of many bird species and the homes of tree and ground animals. The natural environment changed constantly as the different seasons came and went. What I experienced in my youth left me with a strong love of nature and a sense of personal responsibility for good husbandry of the land.

Another joy I remember from growing up on the farm was the birthing of baby animals. I would beg my father to let me help farrow baby pigs on a cold winter night or take care of a newborn lamb or calf. I also learned to harness and work with horses at an early age, and it was an especially exciting time when I was first permitted to go to the field alone and drive a team of horses. Some farm jobs were more enjoyable than others, of course, but seldom do I remember my work as drudgery. Nor was life on the farm all work, and each season brought a different form of recreation. Winter sports were my favorite, but I also looked forward to hot summer days when we were permitted to go barefoot. I loved playing in the creeks on our farm and often would look for—and find—Indian relics. In the fall, my favorite playtime was recess at school.

I was educated at a one-room country school, and many wonderful memories of my teachers and schoolmates, who were also neighbors and friends, remain with me to this day. To reach our rural school, we did not have a road to follow. Instead we crossed two creeks, climbed two hills, and walked through three farmers' land. I remember vividly one clear, crisp fall morning when I heard the voices of three farmers, on different farms, talking to their horses as they harvested their corn crop by hand. I also remember clearly the sound of the corn ears as they hit the wagon bang boards.

Today's agriculture has changed in ways I could never have imagined when I was growing up. We are all aware of the increased size of our farms, the use of improved genetics, the use of chemicals and fertilizers, and the technology of machinery. Livestock production has gone to large-scale operations aided by improved nutrition, livestock confinement buildings, and mechanized feeding and other aspects of animal care. Outside capital has become a big factor in the industrialization and expansion of agriculture as well.

But where are we heading, and what is the future of production agriculture? My answer is rooted in the philosophy of Aldo Leopold. He explained it best in an article he wrote for *American Forests*: "Conservation means harmony between man and land. When land does well for its owner, and the owner does well by his land; when both end up better by reason of their partnership, we have conservation. When one or the other grows poorer, we do not."

My father certainly would have agreed with that statement. His own respect for conservation of the land came from his ancestors and from a passion he had for controlling soil erosion. He lived through the Dust Bowl years of the 1930s, when there was tremendous loss of soil by wind and water erosion. From then on, our farm followed the most innovative and professional soil practices available, and we have worked continuously to make our family farm a model of responsible land stewardship.

Pressure on our natural resources is pushing us from the present age of information technology to a new age of environmental ecology. Iowans face important challenges and responsibilities. In particular, we need to take positive action to maintain clean water in all of our watersheds. The present practice of placing buffer strips and riparian areas along all of our rivers and streams must be expanded. No-till planting, minimum-till planting, contour farming, more scientific use of fertilizer and chemicals and increased research into nonchemical alternatives will also be needed to keep our water systems clean. Likewise, methods of waste management and pasture management must be improved.

Only in recent years have the words "sustainable agriculture" entered our vocabulary. But I realize now that my father's conservation methods fit the current definition of sustainable agriculture. He built some of the first terraces in Iowa, developed structures to prevent stream bank erosion, and practiced a strict crop rotation system. So in the 1930s he was ahead of his time. But other aspects of rural life in my childhood years fit the sustainable agriculture concept too, particularly those related to quality of life and the integrity of the family farm. Increased public demand for a more sustainable food system is accompanying the shift to more environmentally-friendly agriculture practices. As the age of environmental ecology advances, independent family farms need to be on the lookout for new profit-making opportunities that will help them survive in the market place. With rising environmental awareness on the part of the general public, including urban consumers, family farmers may well find they have unexpected allies in their continuing quest to maintain the viability of their rural communities.

David Williams is a semiretired farmer from Villisca, Iowa, who recently served as chairman of the Board of Directors of the Leopold Center for Sustainable Agriculture. He also was one of the early organizers of the Iowa Environmental Council.

CHAPTER THREE
Arts, Tourism & Culture

Sometimes it seems we Iowans are at war with ourselves. Proud of who we are, and what we've created—our families, our communities—at times we seem embarrassed about our state. Nowhere is this more evident than when tourism is discussed. "Why would anyone visit Iowa?"

Well, why indeed? The stories in this chapter make a strong case for Iowa hospitality of the most natural variety. No big theme parks or monuments, the usual fare of the guidebooks. What Iowa has to offer is a quality of life, a relaxed, friendly, accommodating alternative to the hustle and expense of the "name-brand" vacation spots. There are carousels, and county fairs, and Iowa's parks and lakes and river valleys have plenty to occupy everyone in the family.

And as for special treats, which are the focus of the stories in this chapter, there are enough historic restorations, bed-and-breakfasts, bike paths and trail rides, museums and art studios to keep visitors coming back for years to come. Readers will note an absence of involvement by national entertainment corporations in these attractions—and a pronounced local quality to much of what is described. These are local projects, created by community people, and they are eager to share their way of life with visitors.

An Illuminating Business
Bogenrief Studios

Walking into Bogenrief Studios in Merrill feels like entering the business end of a kaleidoscope.

Bits of richly colored glass, beveled and shaped, separated by lead and copper, combine to form lampshades, windows, and ceiling panels. Illuminated from within by warm incandescent bulbs, or from without by the sunlight pouring in the front windows of the studio, these pieces are eloquent and powerful: intricate floral designs, elaborate compositions of people in nature, and "the ladies"—rose-cheeked maidens in flowing gowns, gazing frankly out of their frames, flowers at temple and wrist. These life-sized beauties are inspired by the work of Czech art nouveau painter Alphonse Mucha (1860–1939). Each panel represents two thousand worker-hours of labor.

Mark Bogenrief began working in stained glass in 1978, when he and his wife Jeanne were on strike from a Sioux City packing plant. The strike was a long one. As it dragged on, Mark helped his father, Frank, restore some of the stained glass windows he had bought for resale at his antique store in Hinton, another small Plymouth county town south of LeMars on Highway 75. Intrigued, he read everything he could find about working in stained glass, and began B&B Art Glass in the back of his dad's shop with his twin brother, Nick.

After awhile, the brothers' interests diverged, and Mark began creating large art glass compositions from his home while Nick continued to create smaller, freestanding pieces.

With Jeanne's help, Mark began to sell his work at auctions and shows around the country. Now, twenty-four years later, Bogenrief Studios is one of the best-known, most highly regarded architectural art glass studios in the country—one of only a handful who do their kind of work. The company employs twenty-two people and owns half the business district of Merrill (population 725). Business has increased one hundred times in twenty years, mostly in the past twelve. They have never once advertised.

Not that the studio started out with a splash. For the first ten years, working from their home, the couple produced only the pieces they wanted to make and then peddled them at auctions. It wasn't until around 1991 that they opened the studio to accept custom orders and walk-in shoppers. "The first ten years," says Mark, a big man with a beard, a long ponytail, and a ready laugh, "we had a large garden."

No time now, or need, for home-canning. One of the Bogenrief's pieces can sell at an art auction for $20,000 to $30,000. The shop's goal is to produce one major piece a week. Recently they finished a 12-by-12-foot panel for the owner of a 62,000-square-foot home in Boca Raton, Florida. The largest piece they've completed was a 20-by-40-foot ceiling panel. In addition to orders for new pieces, Mark receives requests to restore damaged antique windows, including a recent one designed by famous Chicago architect Louis Sullivan. The oldest window he's restored was made in 1860.

Mark Bogenrief designed and drew every one of the studio's pieces for the first twenty years. Five years ago, he hired an additional artist. He still picks out all the colors of glass for each piece. (He is particular about those colors. In the basement are thirty tons of leftover scrap glass.) Designs are transferred to paper and laid out on large tables in the workroom. Jeanne, Mark, and their employees meticulously cut the glass to match Mark's design, lay the pieces on the paper, and eventually solder the lead strips together. Lampshades are shaped on fiberglass forms.

month, and during the annual open house up to three thousand people may swarm through the studio in a day and a half.

The Bogenrief's studio occupies three connected storefronts on the south side of Merrill's main street. They were at one time a hardware store, a grocery store, and a manu-facturing business, later used as an auto repair shop. The couple, who share a passion for restoring old buildings, have replaced ceilings, floors, and walls, sandblasted brick, installed bathrooms and lighting, and created a display space in one portion of the studio—all with no outside labor. "We did take a vacation a year or two ago, our first one in eighteen years," Mark says. "We spent the week refinishing the floors in our house in LeMars."

The renovation and expansion at the studio are far from finished. The couple talks with enthusiasm of their short-, medium-, and long-range goals. They recently built a glassblowing facility within the studio which their son Jesse, twenty-seven, and another employee use to produce smaller, more portable "cash and carry" pieces for the growing number of walk-in customers. Bus tours are on the increase, sometimes six or more a

Across the street is the wood studio where two employees create frames for the glass pieces. A block east is a warehouse, right on the highway, where the couple hopes to create a gallery and sculpture garden.

The long-range plan that puts the light in their faces, though, is the dream of creating an artists' colony in Merrill. They have purchased another building, which they intend to convert into apartments for potters and other artists who will share their vision.

During their "free time," of course, there's always work to do on the home place. About a decade ago, the couple bought a large 1906 home in LeMars and have spent countless, loving hours restoring it inside and out. Inside the base of a pink marble porch pillar, they found a metal box—a time capsule placed there by the home's original builders. Letters and photographs had been destroyed by moisture, but two 1906 newspapers were still legible. Mark and Jeanne repackaged them in a waterproof container, adding some memorabilia of their own, and sealed the capsule into the pillar again.

A tour of the couple's home evokes the distinct air of a museum, but one in which each piece has been chosen because it says something special to just the two of them. They have replaced many windows with their own art glass, refinished floors, repapered walls, filled each room with antiques and each wall with pastel oils. Jeanne, willowy and soft-spoken with a beautiful head of silvery-blonde hair, becomes almost reverent when she raises the lid of the large Swiss-made antique music box near the staircase. Strikers decorated with tiny cast-metal butterflies hit the chimes in a precise pattern, and the room fills with century-old music.

"A lady has been in the studio looking at lamps," Jeanne relates. "She says, 'Everyone should have one special thing in their life.' She is choosing one of our lamps to be her special thing."

BIKING WHERE THE TRAINS ONCE RAN
Wabash Trace Nature Trail

When surveyors laid out the route across southwest Iowa for the Council Bluffs–St. Louis Railroad back in the 1870s, they had no idea that they were also preparing a route for thousands of bicyclists and walkers years into the future. Now known as the Wabash Trace Nature Trail, the 62.3-mile-long path, which is named after the second railroad company to use the rails, is the longest rail trail in Iowa and was among the first rails-to-trails projects in the state.

The idea of bicyclists using the route began in the late 1980s when the Iowa Southern Railway, the last of several railroad companies to run trains on the route, stopped running trains on the line. Larry McKern, who owns the Tastee Treat at the trail's northern end and still remembers when trains rumbled by, wondered what would happen to the rail line's right-of-way when the tracks were pulled up.

However, area bicyclists, noting how some rail lines had been converted to bike trails in other states, thought they could do something with what was popularly known as the Wabash Trace. First, though, the land had to be purchased. The Iowa Natural Heritage Foundation (INHF), based in Des Moines, stepped into the picture and purchased the entire corridor. The

bicycling enthusiasts formed an organization, Southwest Iowa Nature Trails, Inc. (SWINT), and took charge of the task of creating a trail out of the torn-up rail bed. That task took ten years and approximately $1.3 million, explains Lisa Hein, Iowa Natural Heritage Foundation's program and planning director. Funding came from the Iowa Department of Transportation and thousands of individual and corporate donors.

The southern half of the trail is currently owned by the Page County Conservation Board and INHF owns the northern portion. SWINT and INHF volunteers partner with other local public and private agencies to provide management assistance.

The first part of the rail route to be converted was its northern end in southern Council Bluffs. The plan was to attract countless bicyclists from the nearby metropolitan areas of Omaha, Council Bluffs, and Bellevue, Nebraska—with an aggregate population of more than half a million people. In bits and pieces over the years, the trail was completed. The last section, a five-mile stretch between Coin and Blanchard on the southern Iowa border, opened in 1997.

Making a railroad into a hike-bike trail was not easy. Trees and brush had to be cut back before work on the rail bed could begin. The route had to be graded, packed, and topped with a layer of finely crushed limestone. Stop signs, posts designed to block motorized vehicles, and rest benches had to be erected. In at least one place, cattle guards had to be installed so a farmer could move his cattle from a field on one side of the trail to a field on the other side.

But the biggest problems in developing the route were the bridges that had been used by the trains. Until they were converted, the Wabash would be nothing but a series of disjointed links scattered across southwest Iowa. At each bridge, planking and side rails had to be built within the framework of the existing structure.

Dan Zollars, who now serves on SWINT's board of directors, was an early advocate of making the Wabash into a hike-bike trail. He used to ride a mountain bike next to the railroad tracks when trains were still running on the line. Dan remembers one bridge that crossed the East Nishnabotna River north of Shenandoah, his hometown. "That bridge had cement pylons that would catch trees, forcing the water to backup into the nearby fields," he explains. "The farmers wanted those out, so we redesigned it to make it a clear-span bridge. On one weekend, over a hundred people were working on that bridge."

Most of the work on the trail was done by volunteers. "The volunteers were good from the start and remain good," says Dan. "Whether it's maintaining the trail or raising funds, they are very committed to working on the Wabash Trace." And these volunteers are not only committed, they are creative. Fundraising events included bike rodeos, haunted hayrack rides, and a radio show. Through these events, they not only raised funds, but built a sense of community around the trail.

"The success of the Wabash Trace Nature Trail comes down to the dedication of the volunteers who have worked on it throughout the years," says Anita O'Gara, vice president of the Iowa Natural Heritage Foundation. "If not for that strong core of volunteers, we would not have gone forward with funding for the project."

Throughout its development, the Wabash has proven to be a strong influence on surrounding areas. When the trail's northern end in Council Bluffs was finished in the late 1980s, it was the only real bike trail in the city. "Now," says John Batt, assistant director of the city's Parks and Recreation Department, "Council Bluffs has about twenty miles of trails that lead from the Wabash. These trails nearly encircle the city and take bicyclists and hikers to Lake Manawa State Park, the levees alongside the Missouri River, the Western Historical Trails Center, and some city parks."

"Our trails were very limited until the Wabash came along," says John. "And now we're planning a $27 million hike-bike bridge to cross the Missouri River and connect our trails to Omaha's."

Over the years, the Wabash Trace has taken on different meanings for bicyclists and others who use it. Near Council Bluffs, horse riders can take their mounts on some stretches of trail, parallel to the main trail, that have been specially prepared for them. Some people use the Wabash for exercise; for others, it's just a fun outing.

Some folks think of the Wabash Trace in terms of eating as well as exercise. At the trail's northern end is Larry McKern's Tastee Treat, where one can sit down to enjoy hamburgers, hot sandwiches, and ice cream treats. Kori Nielsen, a Council Bluffs resident who began riding the trail in 1999, says that groups of people ride the 9.6 miles from Council Bluffs to Mineola on Thursday evenings in the summer to take advantage of Taco Night at the Mineola Steakhouse. At Shenandoah, many bikers leave the trail and ride a few blocks west to the Depot Deli to indulge in the foods there.

Dan Zollars talks about another activity that occurs on the trails—night rides. His favorite section of the trail, on which he rides a Schwinn cross-trainer, is a few miles southeast of Shenandoah where it crosses Tarkio Creek. "The bridge there has a couple balconies, about four-by-twelve feet each, where you can sit," he says. "I like to go down there at night—there aren't any lights around, no vehicle lights from the roads—and I like to watch the meteor showers. And when the lightning bugs are out, they're constantly flashing around you." Dan so enjoyed these outings, that he now helps organize group rides to the Tarkio bridge to watch meteors—especially the Pleides and Perseid meteor showers in August.

VAN BUREN RISING
The Historic Villages of Van Buren County

Enter the rhythm of Van Buren County, where life slows down, residents pride themselves on the utter lack of McDonalds or traffic lights, and progress comes in increments rather than bursts.

In the 1830s, the first settlers to push into the Iowa interior traveled by way of the Des Moines River to the forested hills of what was to become Van Buren County. Here, in the southeastern reaches of the state, steamboats came to ply the Des Moines' waters. Mormon craftsworkers paused to build an enduring style of brick architecture before heading west with Brigham Young's migration. Water-powered industries grew along millstreams to grind the grains of newly cultivated fields, and all the accompanying lawyers and merchants and smiths prospered.

After those first heady decades, settlers gradually pushed further into the state. Rail replaced river, steam, and then gas, and electricity replaced waterpower. Better farmland was found to the north and the west, and floodwaters wreaked havoc. Van Buren County's profile slowly declined, its population dwindled along with income levels, and bustling towns by the 1950s had settled into a collection of small villages with historically charming, benignly neglected edifices. About two dozen of the towns' remaining buildings and homes were built between the 1830s and 1860s.

Few people thought much about what was lost in Bentonsport, which once had a thriving population for the times, but had fallen to fewer than fifty souls. A few, though, thought a great deal about it. Herbert and Burretta Redhead, for instance, believed that Bentonsport's unique architecture could come alive again with tourism, perhaps like an Iowa version of Colonial Williamsburg. The Redheads purchased the Mason House, built by Mormon craftsworkers in

1846 as a hotel for river travelers. They also bought several other buildings in town. By 1969, there was enough support to revitalize Bentonsport that the county's conservation board purchased the riverfront land and several buildings lining Hawk Drive, paralleling the Des Moines River.

Over the years, progress came in fits and starts. Derelict cars and other debris were removed from the riverbanks. Buildings were renovated. A watercolor artist, weavers, a potter, an artisan blacksmith, and a sculptor took up work and residence in Bentonsport, breathing life into surviving buildings. Bentonsport is no Williamsburg, but then again Williamsburg is no Benstonsport.

"Bentonsport is a museum, and all the buildings are artifacts," says Chuck Hanson, who, along with his wife, Joy, now owns the Mason House, which they run as a bed and breakfast. Chock-full of original furnishings, they've opened their home to the community. Oldtimers come by to play bridge in the parlor, retelling stories from their younger days. Guests get a jarful of cookies in their rooms.

As Bentonsport's reputation as an artisan village grew throughout the 1980s and 1990s, it became a reliable tourist draw. Bill and Betty Printy own the Iron and Lace shop, which they built of old barn boards in 1990. It showcases Betty's woven rugs and runners and unique pottery imprinted with the petals of Queen Anne's Lace, and Bill's forged iron creations, such as lamps and intricately detailed pot hangers. Betty, a woman at once elegant and down-home, was raised here. She loves the slow tempo of the old river town.

"It's very quiet here," she says with the faintest hint of southern drawl. "We walk to the river to skip rocks on summer evenings for entertainment. It's better than being in the city, from my point of view."

Renewal didn't end with Bentonsport. Three miles downriver, Bonaparte took notice of its own decline and its neighbor's modest success in the 1980s. Half of Bonaparte's original homes had been torn down, its downtown had become shabby, and in 1986, the sprawling White's Shopping Center—with its groceries, appliances, hardware, insurance, furniture, and clothing—abruptly closed, leaving almost completely empty its line of brick storefronts on First Street. The only bright spot was the Bonaparte Retreat, a popular restaurant in the old Meek's grist mill that had been in business since 1970.

A small group of citizens created a downtown development corporation called Township Stores, Inc. Each investor could contribute a maximum of $2,000; within a month, enough investors had joined to raise $100,000. The corporation quickly went to work refurbishing downtown buildings. The town enlisted technical assistance from the National Main Street Center, establishing a Main Street Program that helped beautify the downtown. Its downtown became the Bonaparte National Historic Riverfront District in 1989.

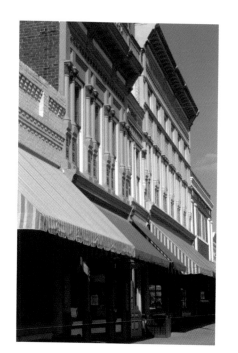

New businesses have steadily blossomed, and only a few stores remain empty. Residents can now buy groceries and hardware, find medical services at a clinic, buy insurance, and get a car repaired without leaving town. Tourists drive in to shop at the many antique stores and browse the hand-made furniture and wood carvings at the Original Woodcarving store.

In 2001, Bonaparte was one of five U.S. towns to receive a "Distinctive Destination" award from the National Trust for Historic Preservation. Strolling down First Street today, past the two historic mills, hearing the roar of the rapids on the Des Moines River, it's easy to forget about the town's decline. Other Van Buren County towns may follow suit.

"Everybody feeds off one another," says Stacey Glandon, past director of the Villages of Van Buren, Inc., which markets the county as a tourism destination. "As one sees success, others want to replicate it."

Such towns have not only pulled themselves up by the bootstraps, but have found cooperating with their neighbors offers advantages. Each village alone may not have enough to support a tourism infrastructure, but strung together, they make a relaxed weekend destination. And with fewer than nine thousand people in the entire county, resources are limited.

"It's not a wealthy county," says Cheryl Duke, manager of the Greef General Store. "We can't squabble—we need everyone united."

Therefore, tourism advertising dollars are pooled. Events—and there is at least one event in the county every summer weekend—are coordinated among villages. October's visitors to the Forest Crafts Festival near Keosauqua can venture out for some beans and cornbread at the Cantril Fall Festival, and then mosey down to Bentonsport for the Arts Festival and browse Bonaparte's flea market.

"So many cities have exactly the same look, the same feel," says blacksmith Bill Printy. "Many small towns have a uniqueness about them, but you can just hear a lot of them gasping their last breaths. Wouldn't it be wonderful if all of our small towns could be thriving little places?"

FROM HORSEBACK RIDING TO STARGAZING

Garst Farm Resorts

When Roswell Garst tried selling hybrid seed corn to farmers in 1929, they thought he might be touched. (Why pay eight dollars a bag for seed corn when you can save your own seed for free?) One agricultural revolution later, his granddaughter Liz Garst is turning Roswell's farm and the land around it into an "agritourism" destination. Some neighbors weren't too sure about her sanity either. (Why would anybody pay good money to stay overnight in an old farmhouse?)

But if history is any guide, the smart money is on the Garsts. Garst Farm Resorts encompasses 4,500 acres of the Raccoon River Valley in west central Iowa, beginning a half-mile east of Coon Rapids on Highway 141. The resort offers so many options for accommodations and activities that it takes a fistful of pamphlets to list them all. The website— www.farmresort.com—explains the resort's mission: to provide all guests a comfortable, entertaining, and authentic experience; to promote the economic well-being of residents living in the Coon Rapids area; and to preserve and protect the resort's beautiful land and the heritage of the Garst Family.

Central to comfort, entertainment, and heritage is Liz Garst, named after her grandmother Elizabeth, Roswell's wife. Liz and her four sisters are conservation

land buyers on the Middle Raccoon River. But it is clearly Liz's vision that drives the resort project.

With a master's degree in rural economic development, a Harvard MBA, and work experience with the World Bank and the Peace Corps, it was natural for Liz to look at the family's land holdings with an eye toward sustainable development. "I have always been interested in rural economic development," she comments, "and I hoped people would want to come here and experience rural Iowa in an authentic way." In support of her hunch—and in tribute to her unflagging effort—Garst Farm Resorts has enjoyed 20 percent growth per year since it opened in 1997.

Guests at Garst Farm Resorts have a variety of options for accommodations. They can stay in the original family farmhouse, now a five-bedroom bed-and-breakfast and the site of the world-famous 1959 visit of Soviet Premier Nikita Krushchev. Other options include the Hollyhock Cottage, formerly a chicken coop; the Oakridge Farmhouse, recommended for small retreats and family reunions; a primitive camping cabin two miles from the nearest road; or several primitive campsites that allow horses.

In addition to solo, family, and small groups of travelers seeking rest and recreation, Garst Farm Resorts accommodates large groups too. Banquet and meeting facilities are available. The resort will cater home-cooked meals to parties of eight or more. The River House Party Facility, a 1900-era barn, is rented out for dances and meetings. "In 1929, people could come to Saturday night barn dances here for twenty-five cents," says Liz. "But the dances were closed down in the Forties for 'moral reasons'—they were selling bootleg Templeton rye."

Horseback trail-riding is the resort's most popular activity. Full-time trail boss Loretta Carpenter leads guests on rides ranging from two to seven hours. But horseback riding is just one of a slew of recreational activities available. Guests can rent canoes to paddle along the Raccoon River or mountain bikes or Gators (John Deere utility vehicles akin to easy-to-operate golf carts) for maneuvering on and off the resort's trails. Fishing enthusiasts have access to twenty ponds stocked with bass, bluegill, and walleye, or to the river for catfish. Guests can take draft horse wagon rides or participate in raptor and falconry workshops. In season, they can hunt white-tail deer with bows or hunt pheasants.

And then there are the guided tours—tours of a nearby commercial farm, of an alternative agriculture operation, prairie tours, botany tours, and a wildlife tour where deer, wild turkey, pheasant, otter, cougar, coyote, beaver, badger, muskrat, and fox have been sighted. And in this part of Iowa, which claims to be one of the darkest spots in the state, the astronomy tour gets rave reviews.

But the most memorable activity at the resort is a personal tour from Liz. With a head for details and a storyteller's rhythm, she reels out tale after tale of the Garst family's history. She tells the story of Krushchev visiting when she was eight; of the acquisition of the resort's timber and prairie and its preservation; of the renovation of the buildings and the addition of recreational equipment. And she tells the fascinating story of how Roswell Garst helped make hybrid seed the future of corn farming.

Liz stresses how crucial the local community has been to the success of the resort, and vice versa. "We have worked hard to get all the neighbors involved with us," Liz explains, navigating a Gator along a section of the resort's eight-mile maintained trail. "The alternative ag tour, raptor and prairie workshops, draft horse wagon rides, wildlife and astronomy tours are all offered by various neighbors on a contract basis." Liz also takes care to point guests toward the nearby community of Coon Rapids, population 1,300, for restaurant dining, golf, bowling, swimming, and shopping.

When this generation of the Garst family is through enjoying the land, Liz says they hope to make a gift of the land to the state of Iowa as the state's largest park.

BUILDING ON A COMMUNITY'S HERITAGE

Manning Hausbarn

In a park on the east edge of Manning stands a time machine.

It's not the whirring, flashing box of 1960s sci-fi movies. It is a much more impressive creation, and three centuries older. It is a meticulously restored German bauernhaus, or farmer's house, a reflection of Manning's proud German heritage and a steadily brightening star in the constellation of small-town Iowa tourist attractions.

The bauernhaus, rechristened a hausbarn by its adoptive community, was built in 1660 in the village of Klein Offenseth in Schleswig-Holstein, Germany. Common to the region in the seventeenth and eighteenth centuries, the structure was built to accommodate both livestock and humans, along with their food, fodder, firewood, and farm implements.

The Manning Hausbarn was donated to the Manning Heritage Foundation by then-owner Claus Hachmann in 1991. Claus had read in his local newspaper of the Schleswig-Holstein descendants in Iowa who were searching for an authentic bauernhaus and was interested right away. His great-uncle Johannes had emigrated to the United States in the 1920s, and American culture and politics had greatly influenced his youth. Donating the hausbarn was, he said, his way of giving thanks.

Standing in a state of disrepair, with a damaged roof and collapsing brick walls, the building was nevertheless inhabited by tenants who had no immediate interest in leaving. German preservationists objected to the loss of a valuable historical relic. Negotiations went on for six years before the building was finally diagrammed, dismantled, packed, and shipped to its new home. It may be the last bauernhaus allowed to leave German soil.

The crates of brick, timbers, and wood pieces remained in storage for more than two years while Manning residents tackled the daunting task of acquiring a site, funding, materials, and manpower to begin reconstruction of the hausbarn. The Manning Heritage Foundation bought a ten-acre tract of land on the east edge of the city, which was the site of a historic farmstead. A meadow on the farm provided an appropriate site for the hausbarn, which had its original home in a pasture.

Five skilled craftsmen, most of them German natives, and a group of area volunteers began reconstruction in July 1999. Within four weeks they had erected the framework, which stands forty-six feet wide, sixty-eight feet long, and forty feet tall. Several of the roof timbers are original, recognizable by their smoke-blackened color. (The family did all of its cooking over an open fire, and the building had no chimney.) One section of the reconstructed hausbarn was created from original brick found stacked, surprisingly intact, in one corner of the building in Germany. Replacement timbers were salvaged from Manning area barns; most are seventy-five to one hundred years old.

A crew of experienced thatchers arrived from Germany in September 1999 to begin creating the roof. They used 6,500 six-pound bundles of reeds, harvested in shallow saltwater marshes in the Baltic Sea. The reeds were wired onto a wooden framework, then molded with a paddle-shaped tool. This authentic seventeenth-century-style roof—still occasionally used in Germany—is expected to withstand the weather for fifty to seventy-five years.

Since the hausbarn began accepting visitors in August 2000, word of the structure's remarkable history and painstaking reconstruction has spread from Carroll County across the globe. The number of bus tours more than doubled from 2001 to 2002. Membership in the Manning Heritage Foundation has multiplied by ten times. The hausbarn has become the centerpiece for community celebrations such as the annual Oktoberfest and German Heritage Day. A new Hausbarn Restaurant and Konferenz Center will open on the site in September 2003.

"What surprises me most about this project is the volunteer commitment," says a member of the Foundation staff. "To get their arms around any project of this scope, people have to be willing to not only do their regular jobs, but pitch in and do extra work to benefit the community. We have one-hundred-plus volunteers working at the park."

$400,000 spent to rebuild the hausbarn, 95 percent stayed in the community. Jobs have been created, and the community hopes to attract related cottage industries to the area. There is talk of a German-American immigrant interpretive center—maybe a motel or two.

But equally important is a feeling, a spirit, around this project. It's not just something to come see, but a vehicle to move people closer together—not just in understanding where they came from and how important that was, but a sense of community pride.

The Heritage Park offers, in addition to the hausbarn, a 1916 farmhouse built in the bungalow style by local banker William Leet, sold a year later to his farmhand Frederick Hassler. The home had indoor plumbing and electricity, unusual for the day. Several outbuildings include a hog house built to accommodate Hassler's highly successful Poland-China hog breeding operation. Hassler's prize boar Checkers sold in 1920 for $20,000. The home is being restored with mission-style furnishings from the period, and clothing, housewares, and other artifacts donated by area families.

The Hausbarn Heritage Park has had a significant impact on this rural community of fifteen hundred. Of the

The Value of Staying Put

Essay by Michael Carey

EMERSON once said, "nothing great is accomplished without enthusiasm." My corollaries are "you'll never preserve what you don't love" and "you'll never love what you don't know." That is why I spent five years studying this southwest part of Iowa that I have come to live in—its land and its people.

One of the conclusions I came to was that if you dig deep enough anywhere, whatever thread you are following will lead directly to "greater happenings" on the world stage. The great Sac and Fox Chief Tecumseh, I found, died in the arms of our Waubonsie. I found Chief Waubonsie's portrait in the Smithsonian. He met with both presidents Polk and Jackson, and his courage and oratory is primarily responsible for the fact that no European settlers were killed here by a Native American. That's quite a legacy.

August Werner, Imogene's eccentric German pioneer who maintained that he was Jesus and spent many years in the Clarinda asylum, also made the first helicopter and actually flew it before the Wright brothers' famous flight at Kitty Hawk. In the asylum files was found a receipt for a working toy model of August's machine big enough to fly cigars "up to Heaven and closer to God." The receipt was made out to Bishop Wright of Cedar Rapids, Orville and Wilbur's father, and was written at a religious convention in Des Moines. The Wright brothers' first attempt at flying, it was also found, was with a machine that was a full-size replica of the toy that their father had bought them seventeen years earlier.

When Iowa ran out of money to furnish its statehouse, it turned for help to August Werner, by then a resident of the Clarinda asylum. Because the old-world cabinetmaker believed he was Jesus, he kept up his carpentry skills.

If you go to the statehouse today, you will see beautiful heavy walnut chests with ornate carved naturalistic handles. August Werner made them.

To think of our governor and legislators all sitting in chairs and at desks made by a man who thought he was Jesus may explain a little something about the political oratory of our fair state.

From my research I wrote *Nishnabotna*, a book of poetry, prose, and dramatic scenes taken from the oral and natural history of the southwest corner of Iowa. From that material I helped write *Dear Iowa*, a musical play for Iowa's sesquicentennial. I was thrilled to see descendants of the very people we wrote about acting out their ancestors' deeds. Interest generated by the play led to the discovery of Chief Waubonsie's grave in the Loess Hills. We have made it our mission to make each new owner of the land aware of this great legacy.

So much can be done with community enthusiasm. Our little corner of the state made the front page of the *Wall Street Journal* by luring the Pella Corporation into Shenandoah *after* the corporation announced a list of finalists for the location of its new plant—a list that had not included Shenandoah. In a town of approximately five thousand, three thousand citizens personally met the company executives in the high school gym, cheered them, and made them feel welcome. When the executives compared the Shenandoah community's enthusiasm to the infighting and negativity in their finalist communities, they decided to go with a small town they hadn't even considered previously. The new plant is here now, and Pella has proven to be a model corporate citizen.

Similar enthusiasm was a factor in raising more than one million dollars to buy the right-of-way of the old Wabash Railroad and creating a sixty-two-mile-long nature trail from Council Bluffs to Blanchard. The trail incorporates some of the last vestiges of native prairie and wild flowers in the state. With haunted trail rides past the graveyard on Halloween, live radio shows, and sales of artwork featuring drawings of scenes along the trail, our small community raised more for trail development than the whole Council Bluffs metropolitan area. It's not size that counts but heart.

For the nature trail fundraising efforts my wife, Kelly, a professional storyteller, researched the old Wabash Railroad and broadcast stories of Iowans' experiences on KMA Radio. She also portrayed Sarah Braunwarth, Iowa's first woman doctor, and Jessie Field, a local community member who was the founder of 4-H. Since then, Kelly has also helped establish the Wabash Trace Fine Arts Camp, bringing approximately 140 young students and about 17 professional artists together for a week every summer. Beautiful color murals done by visiting artists and their camp students now decorate downtown Shenandoah.

I first came to Iowa from the New York City area to attend the University of Iowa's Writers' Workshop. I was amazed to learn how many Pulitzer Prize winners in poetry and fiction over the past fifty years had an Iowa connection. By my count, a full 50 percent had read, taught, or gone to school in Iowa at some time or another. Yet there was no one in the state publishing these authors. They had all gone somewhere else to make it.

"What happened?" I wondered. "Have we lost the ability to believe in ourselves, to credit ourselves? Are we only good if either coast tells us so, if we've made the cover of *Time* magazine?" So for the Iowa Sesquicentennial, I put my money where my mouth was and did an experiment. Along with

Bob Neymeyer of Mid-Prairie Books, I helped found Loess Hills Books, a press dedicated to Iowa fine arts. Loess Hills's first publication was an anthology of Iowa poets—about one-third of the writers were world-famous, one-third were known regionally, and about one-third were just getting started.

Within a month of its publication, U.S. Poet Laureate Robert Hass placed an excerpt from the book on the cover of the *Washington Post*'s *Book World*. The same month, contributor Jorie Graham won the Pulitzer Prize for Poetry. From the proceeds of that book we published four individual volumes of poetry and a memoir, *Change Me into Zeus's Daughter*, by Barbara Robinette Moss. Within months, Barb's book was snapped up by Scribners, and movie rights were sold to Goldie Hawn, with Holly Hunter signed for the lead role. Movie rights for the first novel we planned for publication, Robert Schultz's *The Madhouse Nudes*, were purchased by Francis Ford Coppola's nephew, who is looking to film it for Robert Redford's Sundance Film Festival.

My point here is that nothing would have happened if some *Iowan* hadn't believed in another *Iowan*. From this experience I firmly believe that if we turn to ourselves enthusiastically, because we value what we have, we will preserve what is special, and the glow of that love will attract others. For writers, this means write what you know, and let them come here to admire it. They're looking for something to admire, believe me. Write it, and they will come. Love it, and they will notice. Preserve it, and it will be there for those who come after you.

Michael Carey farms in southwest Iowa. He is a graduate of Lafayette College and the Writers' Workshop at the University of Iowa and is author of five books of poetry.

CHAPTER FOUR
Marketing

In a world where multinational corporations spend millions of dollars on marketing, it seems like small businesses don't stand a chance. But as the stories featured in this chapter show, small businesses can succeed if they are smart about their approach. These marketers rely more on building personal relationships and articulating the values of their products than on flashy advertisements and sales gimmicks. Indeed, in a sense, renewing the countryside is about people building relationships, respecting one another, and providing mutual support.

The marketers in this chapter spur commerce at a community level with the result of building healthy, local economies in our towns, cities, and state. While national and international markets have their place, they have a tendency to obliterate small-scale producers and businesses and the geographical communities they have traditionally served. For the individuals who address the issue in the pages that follow, any sacrifices in potential profits and market share are offset by a quality of life and a degree of personal autonomy that would be impossible to attain elsewhere.

MARKETING VEGETABLES CLEVERLEY

Cleverley Farms

At first glance, Larry Cleverley's farm in Jasper County has not changed much since he grew up down the road fifty years ago.

Old-fashioned purple coneflowers, day lilies, and black-eyed Susans surround a white, two-story farmhouse and dirt lane. Three teenagers arrive, ready to start pulling weeds. Kittens run in and out of a large barn.

But you won't find hogs, cattle, or even an idle combine in the barn. Larry has replaced the corn-and-soybean crops that his grandfather once raised with row after row of vegetable crops, thirty varieties in all, including colorful lettuces, eggplant, garlic, tomatoes, basil, and fourteen kinds of potatoes. In his outbuildings are harvesters, coolers, a refrigerated delivery vehicle, and other tools of the truck-garden trade.

Larry is one of Iowa's largest garlic growers, planting twenty-five thousand bulbs each fall. His forty-five varieties of salad greens—custom-mixed at four dollars per ten-ounce bag—have set new standards at the Downtown Farmers Market in Des Moines and earned him the title of "The Lettuce Guy."

Cleverley Farms, a five-acre organic produce operation, has put the small town of Mingo on the map for farmers market patrons and has helped Larry build a wholesale supply business with some of Iowa's top restaurant chefs. All this has happened since Larry decided at age forty-five to leave a sales career in New York City and move back to the family farm. The rest of the 240-acre farm—about half rolling-timber and half row crops—is rented.

"I wanted to make a living on this farm, but I did not want to incur mountains of debt and sell commodities with prices dictated by factors out of my control," he explains. "I wanted to do something on a smaller scale and try what I had seen in New York City—people connecting with food and the person who produces it."

Larry had seen urban dwellers develop ongoing relationships with farmers-market vendors, their only link to farms and rural life. He also had a friend in the field, a grower who "grew things I liked—and what he did interested me."

Larry returned to Iowa with his wife, Beth, the week before Thanksgiving 1996. He had already planted one hundred pounds of organic German Porcelain garlic—procured in New York—in September to harvest the following summer and had contacted Des Moines restaurants to see what they might buy locally. Larry decided that growing produce organically was the obvious choice and that a white-table-restaurant wholesale business would complement sales at the farmers market.

"Few people had heard of arugula when I first came to the market, but it was starting to become popular on the coasts," he recalls. "At first I took in two pounds a week and often came home with some. Now I sell twenty pounds a week, and we never bring arugula home."

His stand on Court Avenue often has a fifteen-minute waiting line before the market opens. Most people come for the lettuce, mixed for customers depending on how spicy, mild, or colorful they want it. On a typical Saturday, the Cleverleys sell sixty pounds of salad greens every hour.

Other specialty vegetable offerings are available too. Each week Larry sells about 350 pounds of potatoes, including such varieties as Cranberry Red, French Fingerlings, Russian Banana, and Austria Crescent. There are also Korean Red Hot and Music Gourmet garlic, Bull's Blood Chioggia beets, softball-sized Big Daddy sweet onions, and Mammoth Leaf basil with single leaves large enough to hide a fresh tomato.

"My customers are people who like to eat and who like to cook," Larry says.

Recipes for dishes prepared by the restaurant chefs who buy his produce are printed and available for farmers market customers. When business gets slow, Larry tempts onlookers with a taste of something cooked on a portable grill. He suggests how to prepare fresh produce and shares other information about a vegetable's unique flavor or why he decided to grow it.

He even shares his work in the field with those who want it.

In October 1997, Larry traded garlic for labor. Five members of the Iowa State University student organic farm helped him plant garlic bulbs. This initial event has grown into the Garlicpalooza, a social occasion that involves more than 150 customers and friends as the last rite of fall, complete with local foods and wine.

"I wouldn't miss it," said one of his regular customers, a social services manager from Des Moines. "We get to meet other people who want to preserve Iowa's farms. I'm not much of a gardener, but I can say that I plant garlic."

Larry is active in the Taste of Iowa program and promoting Des Moines' Downtown Farmers Market. He is a member of Practical Farmers of Iowa, an association that led him to becoming the Iowa distributor of Niman Ranch meats.

He admits that many Iowans take agriculture for granted and feel disconnected from their food supply because of the emphasis on commodity crops. Although there is nothing magic about farmers markets, once people come, they are often hooked.

"This is all about the food and putting a face on the person who raises that food," he says. "I've just been able to find a nice niche market for specialty crops."

The Cleverleys' farm has been featured in newspapers and magazines, a syndicated garden show, and the television Food Network's "The Best Of" show in April 2002. But Larry hints at a larger source of pride: customer approval. One prominent Des Moines woman introduces him as "my farmer."

"People tell me that I've grown the best garlic they've ever tasted," Larry says. "But my father, who had farmed for more than fifty years, once told me that he had never had anyone tell him that he raised the best pork they had ever tasted. We want people to know where their food comes from, and that is one of the things we are trying to do as we reinvent agriculture and reestablish local food systems."

INCUBATING STAY-AT-HOME BUSINESSES

Franklin County Cottage Industries

Cathy Carlson knew she had a talent for cake baking and decorating. Back in 1978, she was hoping to turn her talent into income with a "stay-at-home" business while being a "stay-at-home" mom for her newborn daughter. Mixing cake batter, swirling frosting flowers, and child rearing from her home in rural Hampton, Iowa, was a rewarding blend for Cathy, until the late 1980s.

"I had figured out what I was good at, what the community needed, and the cake decorating business was going really well at first," says Cathy. "Then during the farm crisis people stopped ordering decorated cakes. But I wasn't giving up on my business. I felt like I had to find other opportunities."

"I added all kinds of cookies and bars made from scratch to my business," Cathy explains. "Now I'm making my money from the basic chocolate chip cookie!"

There were more than sugar and chocolate chips stirring around in the Carlson kitchen. Cathy, a longtime member of the Hampton Area Chamber of Commerce, was putting together some ideas—thinking about other folks in the area who were trying to make an income from home businesses. To be a better businessperson herself, she took a leadership course—Iowa State University Extension's Tomorrow's Leaders Today. Part of that course was a class project, and Cathy zeroed in on the area's cottage businesses.

Cathy started watching what people purchased at grocery stores and a nearby truck stop and what the retailers had to offer. People were buying sweets— and she knew that she had a talent for baking cookies and bars. So to her Cakes! Cakes! Cakes! business, she added "and More!"

"I saw other folks in the area trying to make an income from home businesses and began thinking about the benefits of coming together," Cathy explains. "I approached the Hampton Area Chamber of Commerce and started an effort to organize all those home and cottage businesses."

Pat Sackville was the new Hampton Area Chamber director in 1992 when Cathy came to her. Together they identified 150 local home-based businesses. The large number in their database prompted them to more clearly identify the type of businesses that they were targeting. They defined cottage industries as ones offering products or services manufactured in the home and ones with no national brand affiliation. Cathy and Pat began talking to these people—crafters and candle-makers, gardeners and lawn care specialists, and others—at community meetings, craft shows, and county fairs.

Linda Dow was just getting her dried flower arrangement and greenhouse plant business going when she went to a meeting in Dows that Cathy had organized.

"They were good people with a good plan for organizing local cottage businesses into a group called Franklin County Cottage Industries," says Linda. "I became a member of the group. Belonging has kept my business going and growing."

"Every county has lots of skilled artisans. It takes time to locate them and organize them, but it is worth it," says Avis. "Franklin County Cottage Industries brought us all together and helped us build a very strong network."

Judy Wrolson calls the networking that has been created by Franklin County Cottage Industries "phenomenal" and something that she experiences on a daily basis. She was crafting fabric and designing note cards and gift bags in her Hampton home under the business name Peacock House Designs when she joined Franklin County Cottage Industries.

"The educational opportunities that came with belonging to the group have been invaluable. I would not have been this successful without the things I learned," says Judy.

Cathy says the group, which now has eighteen active business members, was organized on a few simple premises. As a group, she felt they could build public awareness of their businesses. By working as a unit, they could provide support for each other as they faced common challenges. They could develop marketing strategies as a group that would increase sales. By virtue of the number of them working together, they would be taken more seriously as business people.

Avis Johnson was selling jams, jellies, and sewn-craft items at craft fairs, and she was sewing items for friends and family as a hobby. Then a combination of her retirement and friendship with Cathy encouraged her to think along the lines of being a business.

The group started with each business contributing an equal amount of funds into the pot. Because they are a Hampton Area Chamber of Commerce subcommittee, the Chamber manages their funds, provides administrative duties for the group, and connects them with other resources.

A Cottage Industries parade of homes was held each fall for the first five years, greatly increasing awareness of the group and of the individual businesses. At the same time, monthly meeting "lessons" related to home-based businesses were getting the group going.

"We had experts talk to us about efficient use of our home space, bookkeeping, tax issues, marketing, merchandising, and web design," explains Cathy. "We could plan a year's worth of meetings and at the end easily recognize the ways we had grown."

As they put each lesson into practice and found success, they wanted to learn more. Cathy, Avis Johnson, and Linda Dow took a small business course called Fast Track. Judy Wrolson met regularly with staff from North Iowa Area Community College's Small Business Development office.

"I had been a bookkeeper for years, but the Fast Track class taught me how to make a business plan and walked me through step-by-step planning," states Avis. "It was very, very helpful and I wouldn't have considered taking it if I hadn't been part of Franklin County Cottage Industries."

The others also credit this learning experience with boosting their entrepreneurial growth.

"Franklin County Cottage Industries has become an incubator for local home businesses," says Cathy. "As part of this group, we have gotten our feet on the ground. We have learned and grown at a steady, but individual, pace. Some of us have grown to the point of adding Main Street stores to our businesses. Avis is selling some of her products on geezer.com, and we have a co-op gift store set up at the truck stop."

Cathy has seen her business grow from Cakes! Cakes! Cakes! and More at her home to include Cathy's Country Cook'n in Latimer. Linda continues to start plants in her Down to Earth greenhouse on her farm and has expanded into the flower shop in Dows with cut flowers, plants, and gifts. Judy, still creating Peacock House Designs products in her home, has opened Cornerstone Cottage, which features her handcrafted items and those of thirty-five other local consignors, along with a few unique items she gets from market.

Franklin County Cottage Industries has had a positive ripple effect on other area businesses. Judy's store provides a selling spot for many local artisans. Area gift shops and eateries are contacting members for their products. The group's success continues to generate interest.

"Franklin County Cottage Industries has been a nurturing organization," says Judy. "We look out for each other; we know each others' needs and make connections for one another when we come across resources. There have been great benefits being affiliated with the Chamber of Commerce and having Pat Sackville's guidance." Pat, who continues as Chamber director and is now Hampton mayor, sees this core group of businesses as a great resource for beginning area cottage industries.

"What a wonderful time to come into this group," she says. "With all the expertise from personal experience and applied learning, these people are a wealth of information. They have given much to the area's cottage industry, and I expect that will be extended to retail business now that some are moving to Main Street."

Cathy Carlson's little girl has grown up. She works part time for Cathy, and now she's a mom. Like Cathy, she's wondering what talent or interest she might turn into a business so she too can be a "stay-at-home" mom with a "stay-at-home" business.

MILK WITH A REPUTATION
Radiance Dairy

A California resident on a repeat visit to Iowa is met at the airport by a friend. As they drive to the friend's home in Fairfield, the visitor asks, "Would you stop at the grocery store? I'd like to get some Radiance Dairy whole milk." The driver laughs and responds, "I knew you were coming. The refrigerator is stocked!"

We have all seen countless advertisements like this for countless products. But this time there's a twist, it's not an ad—it's real life, and it's a scene that is played out over and over in this particular town for this particular glass of milk.

"We hear stories like that all the time. It's kind of humbling to hear them. A lot of people say they can't drink any milk but ours," Radiance Dairy owner Francis Thicke matter-of-factly states. The irony is that despite testimonials that would make a New York ad writer swoon, Francis does little traditional marketing. "A lot of marketing in this country is making people want what they don't need. I'm really opposed to that," Francis says.

So if it's not the media ads, what is it that makes Fairfield residents—and visitors—go out of their way for Radiance Dairy milk? There are several answers to that question. The most obvious one is the unique consumer marketplace in Fairfield. Radiance Dairy produces all organic products and in this town, populated by an estimated three thousand adherents to Transcendental Meditation, that has an appeal all its own. To meditators, the quality of the food one consumes is considered as important as daily meditation. Everybody's, the local natural foods store, is thriving, and the town's two mainline grocery stores have large organic food sections.

Yet the Radiance appeal goes beyond the boundaries of the meditator community. "We always assume that we don't have much of a name outside the meditator community, but then we'll get introduced to people who are not in that community and we'll be surprised that they buy our product," says Susan Thicke, Francis's wife and business partner. The product sells well in the local Hy-Vee and EconoFoods, and they receive persistent requests to ship regionally.

But Francis and Susan are local producers and they like it that way. They have dedicated themselves to customer satisfaction at the local level and have been rewarded with staunch customer loyalty, a loyalty that has helped the business thrive.

Originally from southeastern Minnesota, the Thickes bought their dairy business and its twenty-two cows in 1992 and relocated them to what had previously been a conventional corn-and-soybean operation. "There was nothing here but the corn crib out there," says Francis, pointing to the south. The first thing the Thickes built was a processing facility, which they lived above for the first four years. Clearly business has been good. Now they live comfortably in a gracious, new two-story home overlooking the lush pastures upon which the cows graze.

Francis and Susan remain faithful to Radiance Dairy's local roots. "Philosophically, we want to focus on servicing a local area. It takes a quantum leap to serve a regional market. We prefer something where we can control the quality," Francis says.

Francis attributes the quality of the milk's flavor to the Jersey cattle in his herd. The milk just plain tastes good, an attribute of Jersey milk, Francis says. Because Jersey milk is higher in milk solids, it carries a lot more body and is more satisfying. But add to that the health benefits that come from

pasture-grazed cows. "People who have had milk allergies all their lives say they can drink our milk," Francis says.

Although careful not to make health claims, Francis points to recent research on the health benefits of the milk fat of grazed cows. According to studies conducted by the University of Wisconsin, pasture grazed cows produce up to 500 percent more of the anticarcinogen Conjugated Linoleic Acid (CLA) in their milk than confined cows.

In a world where a cow in a conventional dairy operation rarely catches sight of a fresh blade of grass, Radiance Dairy cows are treated to fresh pasture after every milking. Pasture grazing has gained Francis Thicke celebrity far beyond the Fairfield city limits, and he is a frequent speaker on rotational grazing at sustainable agriculture conferences and farm demonstration workshops. He and his brother Art, who operates the La Crescent, Minnesota, home farm where they grew up, have developed a body of knowledge based on a combination of readings and observations. At its heart is the belief that the farm is an ecosystem, and the wise farmer will work to understand and protect its integrity.

For the Thickes, that requires working with natural processes. "The farm is an organism. You should be careful of what kind of energies or products are brought onto the farm or are taken off because you really have an organism here and you want it to grow with its own integrity," Francis explains.

An indicator of soil health is the number of organisms living in it, earthworms being one. In the first years when he was transitioning the land away from conventional fertilizers, Francis says he could kick over twenty or thirty dried-up cow patties in the spring before finding an earthworm. Now, he finds thirty to fifty earthworms under each one; "It's really come a long way," he says.

To build the strength of the farming ecosystem, Francis strives to increase the plant and animal diversity. Planting a rich diversity of forages, from grasses to chicory to clovers, he now sees a lot of birds he had never seen on the farm before. He takes satisfaction in the fact that when Extension workers held a field day on his farm recently, they did some soil sampling down in the pasture. They were impressed that where the pH was 5.6, the clovers were thriving, and there appeared to be a robust cycling of nutrients.

Restoring the health of the farm's natural ecosystem has taken time, and so has the marketing of the Radiance Dairy product. An apprentice farmer hoping to learn the secret of the dairy's success may be surprised to learn that there really is very little marketing involved. As Francis tells it, "Most people have the idea that if they produce a product, they have to market it. I have the idea that if it's really a product that people want, maybe it's slow, but word of mouth is the way to sell it. We've done just fine letting it go by word of mouth, and we're happy with that."

RELATIONSHIP MARKETING IN SOUTHWEST IOWA

Audubon County Family Farms

Audubon County lies in southwest Iowa midway between Des Moines and Omaha. It is one of the smaller counties in Iowa, but contains a full range of topography—from gently rolling hills in the northeast section to flat expanses and river bottoms, to the steeper hills in the southwest corner.

Historically, it has been among the top ten counties in livestock production, and it also was home to a thriving dairy industry until the dairy buyout program in the middle 1980s. Today, farming in the county has come to resemble the prevailing pattern in Iowa: commodity corn-and-soybean production, cattle feeding, and industrialized swine production.

The landscape reflects these changes. As farmers have retired or quit farming, farms have been consolidated and farm units have become larger. Both rural and community populations have declined and their demographic profiles have aged as young people leave for school or jobs. Empty and decaying farmsteads dot county roads. Communities in Audubon County are struggling to maintain their retail bases.

It is against this background that a group calling itself Audubon County Family Farms was conceived and developed as a marketing cooperative for agricultural products. Growing out of a 1997 Iowa State University Extension Rural Action program, it initially included the county Cattlemen's Association, the Pork Producers, and agriculturally related businesses along with farm families. Soon the composition of the group narrowed to include just small- to midscale family farmers that were looking for new ways to market their products.

Today, Audubon County Family Farms continues as a group farm operation that collectively produces pork, chickens, eggs, honey, beeswax candles, apples, cherries, and greenhouse tomatoes. Because the group's structure is flexible and open to new members, the makeup of the membership and the products offered can change.

There are no rigid guidelines restricting membership and the products that are marketed, but, as the group's name indicates, it is geared toward true small to midscale, independent farming operations. An effort is made to only offer products produced in an environmentally sensible manner—for example, hogs raised in straw-bedded hoop houses instead of confinements.

In 1998, Cindy Madsen, one of the members, took on the role of marketing for the group. During the growing season, she makes weekly trips to the Des Moines Downtown Farmers Market and also sells products locally.

Audubon County Family Farms has gone through several metamorphoses since 1997, both in conception and composition. It continues to be an important marketing outlet for its members. From the beginning they have worked to develop the notion of relationship marketing—trying to establish connections between customers and producers. This effort has required education and time—beyond that of the actual transaction. Customers who purchase the group's products have an opportunity to learn how the products are raised and to come to know the producers. Members who sell products get to know customers' concerns and preferences.

Besides being a useful marketing tool, relationship marketing is immensely satisfying. Urban and local customers become acquainted with producers and can find connections to rural Iowa. Those who produce the bounty from Audubon County come to know the folks who purchase and use it. It is a relationship that sustains and renews both sides.

COME MEET THE PEOPLE WHO GROW YOUR FOOD

Des Moines Downtown Farmers Market

Every Saturday morning from May through October ten thousand people head for downtown Des Moines with one thought on their mind: experiencing Des Moines' Downtown Farmers Market. Here, in an invigorating blend of commerce and conviviality, shoppers are guaranteed a vast variety of Iowa-grown goods, and farmers a congregation of customers.

Each Saturday, people of all ages mill past vendor after vendor offering everything from bison meat to chemical-free tomatoes, together with a generous sprinkling of arts and crafts and a lively dash of music. A tiny tots train toots through the street, packed with preschool kids. Lilting Irish tunes lift the spirit on one street corner, jazz riffs on another. A series of umbrellaed tables provide rest for families, and a quiet place to read and sip a morning cappuccino for others.

"The homemade products are really nice, you know. The bakeries from the south side, the family-made products, I like those things," explains Vicki Wagner of Clive on her weekly shopping trip with her daughter Heather. "I like the things you can't get by going to Dahl's or Hy-Vee. And it's just a nice atmosphere."

Bill and Judy Lemosy from Pleasant Hill dismount from their bicycles, having already ridden twenty-five miles. "This is a different kind of shopping experience," they declare. "It's a lot more fun!"

That experience is what makes the Downtown Farmers Market so successful, says Kelly Foss, director of special events for the Downtown Community Alliance, who manages the market. "People who come to the Downtown Farmers Market come for people watching, to meet their friends, to listen to the music. But you know, they could do that at the mall, really, if you think about it. But they do it at the farmers market for the experience. They enjoy the 'outdoorsness' of it and the briefness of it because it only happens once a week and only during the growing season."

The exuberant camaraderie of shared experience is a defining element of the market. This is something vendors as well as shoppers enjoy doing together. Emmack Farms and Shepard's Gardens, both from Colfax, Iowa, share three vendor spaces. Elmer Shepard explains, "Delmar Emmack and I worked together at Maytag years ago. I'm retired, but Delmar still works and he's got his farm." Another family friend from Urbandale joins them on occasion. "It keeps us busy and it keeps us young," says Mary Emmack.

In the Lee family, who came from Thailand fifteen years ago, everyone participates, from preparing food on Friday night to running food stands on Saturday morning. Yia Lee, a recent graduate of a Des Moines high school, mans a small Asian food stand, while brothers, sisters, cousins, and friends joke playfully nearby. Yia's aunt runs Mao's Eggroll up on the corner. An uncle sells pretzels a block away.

The owner of Dancing Lady Gardens is Sha5on Nelson ("I have a silent 5 in my name. When I get to be 60, I'll have a silent 6. No reason your name shouldn't tell how old your are."), who shares two spaces with Amy Plymat.

For these longtime friends, the farmers market is something they like doing together. Sha5on specializes in unusual perennials. She also designs, manufactures, and sells garden stakes, most in fanciful fairy themes. Amy sells culinary herbs, both fresh cut and potted. "I sell the plants so people can grow their own bouquets," she says. During the winter, Amy has an import business, scouting the Netherlands for ladies scarves, which she sells to museum shops and ladies clothing stores. "I used to have a health food store, but I really don't like that whole fixed-overhead thing; you're a prisoner," she says.

It's a sentiment echoed by Darwin Thede, owner of Pappy's Popcorn. "This is the ideal outlet for vendors that do the sorts of things that you see down here," he says. "You eliminate having to be open every day of the week. It just works out much better that you have an intense crowd for a half day and then you're done 'til next week." Friends help Darwin sell his kettle corn in turn for help he gives them during the week. "It's fun and productive, and we meet a lot of people," Darwin says. "That's really the fun of it. We always see the same people. They enjoy coming down."

The farmers market is also a place where you can learn a little something. "We chose to be off the beaten path because it gives us a chance to talk to people," Sha5on explains. "People have questions and ask, 'Can I do this?' You'll get people with every sort of sophistication level, from people who know nothing to people who are bringing textbooks in with them."

"People like to meet the farmer or person who grows the food they eat," says Debbie Shimer, who runs Heartland Gardens in New Virginia with her husband, Tom. "We base our sales on relationship marketing. We let people know we grow everything we sell. People ask, 'Did you grow this?' or 'Does it have chemicals on it?' and we share information. Tom has been talking about the garlic for the past couple of weeks. When to plant it. When to harvest it. Our customers are curious." But the information sharing goes both ways, Debbie adds, "Many people have been gardening for years, and we learn from our customers also."

The market is a place where children can learn too, Kelly, the market manager, explains. "When people come here, they bring the whole family, so having an activity for kids enhances the experience."

In a booth sporting the sign "Earn your Ph.B." (for Pioneer Hi-Bred, the market's sponsor), kids learn something different each week about growing things. "The activities are focused on agriculture and the environment," Kelly explains. "We want the kids to meet some farmers and to think about where their food is coming from." One Saturday, in an activity titled "Play with Your Food," the kids did food sculpture, and then ate it. On Mother's Day, they planted flowers in a cup for their moms and talked about how water and sun helps the flowers grow. On another week, they drew imprints of leaves while a teacher talked with them about the trees in their neighborhoods. "It gets kids thinking about their environment," Kelly explains.

The success of the market comes from maintaining the right balance of product offerings, Kelly asserts. "Our number one desired vendor is an Iowa farmer who grows and sells their own products," she says, and they account for at least 80 percent of the 150 vendors who attend each week. The remaining vendors are a mix of crafters or people who offer prepared foods, such as breakfast pizzas or an array of unique ethnic food. Live musicians add to the atmosphere.

Market success depends on the skill of the market manager and the ability of organizers to respond to the unique demands and interests of their community, according to Barbara Lovitt, marketing specialist with the Iowa Department of Agriculture and Land Stewardship's Bureau of Horticulture and Farmers Markets. "You need to find an approach that's right for your community," she says. "And it usually takes five years for a market to get out of the 'toddler' stage." Education, she says, is vital. The Bureau provides an annual workshop and a quarterly newsletter to provide technical assistance and publishes a Market Fresh Directory each year. "Generally speaking, the stronger the manager and the more adaptable the organization, the more successful the farmers market is going to be."

Marketing as Conversation

Essay by Mary Swalla Holmes

Iowans are nice. We smile at strangers and say "please" and "thank you" to convenience store clerks. Friends who move here from big cities find it hard to believe that we mean it when we say "stop over sometime." This supportive and helpful culture is rooted in the interdependent relationships that characterize Iowa's small farming communities.

During the first seventy-five years of white settlement, Iowans depended heavily on each other for food, shelter, and labor, just as native peoples had for centuries. The countryside was dotted with small farms that provided the growing communities with fresh eggs, creamy butter and milk, and meat and vegetables. Securing meat or eggs often meant a trip to a neighbor's farm for a visit and a piece of cherry pie. A deal might have been struck to barter labor or skills, or cash may have exchanged hands. Whatever the medium of change, this local economy was built on mutually beneficial relationships. The yearly output of the farm was designed to match the needs of the community it served.

Then came the industrial revolution and, along with it, new ideas for agriculture. A few powerful men amassed great fortunes by importing cheap labor to work in the mines, build the railroads, and fuel the factories. Cities grew, and industrial economies emphasized profits rather than people's everyday needs. Production was driven by market factors, not relationships. Individuals became cogs in the wheels of industry, interchangeable and replaceable. Long hours of hard labor tore families apart and destroyed the relationships that built neighborhoods. Laborers were paid so little that cheap food was all they could afford.

Conditions improved gradually in the twentieth century, thanks to government policy changes, union demands, and other factors. But improvements came at considerable cost to rural America, for industrial agriculture emerged as the principal means of feeding the cities. Farmers were encouraged by the industrial sector—and to a considerable extent by government policy as well—to get bigger and more efficient, to buy more land and more machinery, and to produce more and more.

By the 1970s, industrial agriculture had reshaped the countryside, and farmers were planting from fence row-to-fence row to meet demand. In addition, farmers had become caught up in national and international business cycles that left them vulnerable to market prices that sometimes fell below their costs of production. Ultimately, in the 1980s, prices fell so low that many farmers went broke. Corporate business leaders and their political supporters saw this cycle as unfortunate but inevitable, saying this was the way modern economies worked.

A few Iowans refused to take the path of industrial agriculture, choosing instead to create new marketing systems for a new agriculture. These hearty souls chose to maintain the relationships that bound them to their communities and to their land. They endured the scoffing of their neighbors in the 1970s, when prices were high, and then stepped forward to comfort the same neighbors who lost everything in the 1980s. Today, their tenacity is paying off, and they are offering a model of hope and health to the world.

Many of these farmers joined organizations of like-minded individuals. Practical Farmers of Iowa (PFI) began as a small group of farmers who saw the need to do things differently. In the beginning, their emphasis was on production practices, such as ridge-tilling to save the soil and recycling nutrients to protect water supplies. But before long, they were also redefining the market system by developing direct markets to capture the value of the high-quality foods they were producing on their farms.

These farmers learned to see the world as a set of relationships, and that perspective changed every aspect of their lives. The result is healthier families and healthier communities, as well as healthier soil. PFI and many other grassroots organizations continue to grow and thrive in Iowa, building an economy that supports families and communities and the environment.

Another grassroots organization that focuses on relationship marketing is the Iowa Network for Community Agriculture (INCA). This group actively fosters relationships between farmers and consumers, particularly through community supported agriculture (CSA). CSA members invest directly in a farm or group of farms and receive a variety of products as a return on that investment. This provides members with high-quality food and a direct connection to the farmer and the land. The farmer benefits by securing a stable market and linking with a supportive community that shares some of the risks of the farming enterprise. Many of these farmers also sell produce at farmers markets and to local institutions.

The Leopold Center for Sustainable Agriculture is another key Iowa institution promoting innovation in marketing systems. Created by the Iowa General Assembly as part of the 1987 Iowa Groundwater Protection Act, the Leopold Center's mandate is to contribute to the development of profitable farming systems that conserve natural resources. The Center has supported innovative research and groundbreaking marketing projects for a decade and a half now, and its work has had a pronounced impact on the way people think about agricultural opportunities in Iowa.

In particular, the Leopold Center has led the effort in Iowa to link farmers to local institutions, such as schools and hospitals. Pilot projects have helped farmers identify new—and often readily available—markets and to bring together diverse partners to address these marketing opportunities. Currently, the center is facilitating a working group to identify issues that affect farmers building niche markets for pork.

While many other state agencies and institutions voice support for these small but growing marketing opportunities, in reality only a tiny fraction of the Iowa's resources are devoted to this work. For the most part, the state's vast economic infrastructure is designed to support industrial agriculture—which provides cheap commodities to increasingly unreliable global markets. Yet even as the social, moral, and environmental consequences of industrial agriculture erode the very heart of our state, fear of change often paralyzes our institutions.

In small pockets of activity, however, change is happening organically. New networks are forming, made up of farmers and consumers who share a belief that healthy food and healthy food production are the basis of a healthy life, not a luxury or a novelty. Built on strong Iowa traditions of community relationships, these networks will continue to grow in the years ahead, nourished by the honest, hardworking, *nice* people of Iowa.

Mary Swalla Holmes promotes sustainable community development through her work in local food systems development and by writing about her life experiences in rural Iowa.

CHAPTER FIVE
Product Innovations

The innovative men and women profiled in the pages that follow are risk takers, first and foremost. They have put their time and their money on the line in the belief that people will buy their products—even when, at first, people aren't sure what a particular product is or how it should be used. Thus they have often doubled as educators, patiently dispelling myths and correcting misinformation, waiting for that "a-ha!" moment when the restless skeptic becomes a paying customer. The Grinnell tofu manufacturer, the Woodward goat-cheese producers, the Indianola wine maker—these and many other Iowa risk takers have known the thrill of buyer and seller finding one another for the first time.

Among the stories in this chapter are descriptions of manufacturers and retailers who have gone out on a limb getting something brand new out on the market. Many innovators have had the help of local and state agencies—chambers of commerce, Iowa State University Extension, the Iowa Department of Agriculture and Land Stewardship, and the U.S. Department of Agriculture—in getting started. But these are support services, for ultimately the burden has been borne by individuals and families willing to take a big chance on something they believed in.

IOWA'S GOAT CHEESE PIONEERS
Northern Prairie Chevre, LLC

As the first licensed farmstead goat cheese processors in Iowa, the three women of Northern Prairie Chevre, LLC are truly pioneers. When Kathy Larson, Connie Lawrance, and Wendy Mickle launched their company in January 2000, they found themselves in new territory. Every step was a discovery. But rather than being daunted, they were challenged. "We thought, the greater the risk, the greater the reward," says Wendy.

The company grew from a simple pleasure: love for goats. "Kathy and I had been raising goats for about eleven years. We purchased them as cute animals and great pets, with wonderful personalities," remembers Wendy. But the herd grew, and the women reached a crossroads. "We said, 'OK, if this is going to be a hobby, we can't get any bigger. It has to start paying for itself, or we'll have to start scaling back.'"

"When we networked with Iowans who raise goats, we found that they were sending their milk to Wisconsin to be processed into cheese, and then shipping it back to Iowa. We sort of raised our eyebrows and said 'There's an opportunity here,'" remembers Wendy.

The three women pooled their money. And then the research—and ambiguity—began. They discovered that the state of Iowa had interpreted its regulations for large commercial companies but not small farmstead businesses. They discovered equipment was hard to find. They discovered they needed to develop their own recipes for cheese. They discovered why they were the state's first on-farm goat cheese producers.

"We discovered why people are dissuaded," says Wendy. "There wasn't anybody to ask questions of; nobody was doing it. Each state has its own set of pasteurization regulations in conjunction with the federal government. We were asking questions, and the state wasn't quite sure where to put us. We didn't fit the mold."

The women plunged ahead and began to find answers and allies. They transformed the garage on Kathy and Wendy's farm into a production kitchen and built a room in the barn for a sanitary location for milking. They found a French-made stainless steel bulk tank from a Canadian distributor, and a local bank provided a loan for the equipment. "As we have developed, we have found the state inspectors to be allies," notes Wendy. "To ensure our products are safe, they test our milk on a monthly basis, and all of our products, as well as our facilities, are inspected regularly."

The trio quickly began building a reputation for their mouthwatering cheeses, and in 2001 sold approximately 2,200 pounds of cheese. Their main outlet is the Des Moines Downtown Farmers Market—one that the women say they couldn't do without. "If there hadn't been such a strong market in Des Moines, we would have reconsidered our endeavor," says Wendy.

The timing was also right. "It's a time when Iowans are wanting to know what they're eating, where it's coming from, and who's preparing it," says Wendy. In addition, goat's milk cheese was increasingly finding its way into recipes presented by TV chefs and popular gourmet magazines.

Their second most important market is local restaurants. For example, David North, the chef at Hotel Pattee, the four-diamond hotel in Perry, uses cheese from Northern Prairie Chevre almost every day. "Their cheese is very rich and very creamy. I always have a couple of tubs of their chevre on hand, and theirs is the only feta that I use," he says. Popular menu items include a spinach and strawberry salad with feta cheese, and a stuffed chicken breast with chevre and portabello mushrooms. "I even slipped it into macaroni and cheese," Chef North reported. "People were saying, 'Man, this is good!'"

The versatility of the cheese makes it particularly appealing, say the women. Although consumers delight in spreading the herbed chevres (including garlic chive, garlic basil, summertime salsa, and Italian blend) on crackers and bread, they also enjoy ideas for new recipes, and ways to use the variety of cheeses. The Queso Blanco, a spongy, crumbly cheese is good on pizza, salads, and even cut into cubes and fried. The crispy cheese is great with scrambled eggs and salsa. "It can be an appetizer, entrée or dessert, lunch or breakfast. That's what's most appealing. People are getting more in tune with sharing food as a form of entertainment and socializing," says Connie.

In addition to the tangy feta and creamy chevre, the company makes fresh cheddar curds, Parmesan, and an aged farmhouse cheese. "Our cheeses are all made from the same milk," explains Connie. "The differences come from the cooking temperatures, the starter cultures, the curdling agents, how much you stir it, and whether or not it's pressed or molded. Our milk is cooled and used quickly, within a couple of days, for best flavor and consistency."

Goat's milk is similar to cow's milk in many ways, but is substantially higher in vitamins A and B, and riboflavin. Also, it is easier to digest than cow's milk. Fatty acids found only in goat's milk add to its rich flavor and nutrition and inhibit cholesterol deposit. "Healthy food is appealing to people," says Wendy.

Also appealing is the knowledge that the three "goat moms" (the owners' email nickname) love every one of their sixty-plus goats. A visit to their beautiful, secluded farm near Woodward, Iowa, confirms that the herd is cared for with a special brand of affection. Only sixteen goats are milked. The rest

are kids, a few bucks, and retired grandmas that the three women can't bear to part with. The goats are a Nubian breed, chosen for their exceptionally rich milk. Their long floppy ears make them look rather like a cross between a deer and a beagle. And, in fact, the women say they act much like dogs. "The babies behave like puppies," says Wendy. "They are very smart. They love you, wag their tails, love to be scratched, and learn their names."

And yes, every one of them has names. There is Ellie May, Phoebe Baby, Hannah, Miss Tilly, Macy, Fancy, Lucy, and Lacy. There's Mav, Dora, Velvet, Beatrice, Nellie, Jubillee, and Penelope. "Each one is different," says Wendy. The goats, eager for attention, peer over the fence, and Wendy plants liberal kisses on their heads, and scratches them under their furry chins. "We have one here who smiles. Can you smile for us, sweetie?" she asks one of the larger goats, who sports a dramatic grin.

The women have developed their own recipe of high quality grain mixture. "The girls tell us if we come up with something they don't like; they just won't eat it," says Wendy. No chemicals or hormones are added to the food. The animals are kept healthy through basic inoculations. Kids are bottle-fed milk that has been milked from their mothers and pasteurized. Doing so keeps the kids healthier and ensures a stronger bond with humans, the women explain. Two Great Pyrenees dogs help keep the herd safe from coyotes.

The three friends have discovered that running their own business means that they must simultaneously be cooks, producers, marketers, and distributors. On a given day, they might help deliver a kid, try out a new recipe, fix the caulking on the milk house, meet with a restaurant owner, and sell cheese at a farmers market. "There are three of us, and we can divide the work three ways," says Wendy. "We still chase our tails on some days, but this year it's a lot easier. We're pretty pleased. Things are smoothing out."

THE AESTHETICS OF TOFU
Wildwood Harvest Foods

Visit Tom and Alesia Lacina's farm in Grinnell, Iowa, and you will see beauty everywhere. A lush green hedge hems in a slightly rambunctious flower garden on the grounds of their rust-brick family home. Their younger son, Jon, plays in the yard with their dog. Nearby is Tom's father's woodshop—smelling deliciously of shavings and wood finish—and through a door in the shop is Alesia's art studio, full of colorful canvases painted by both Alesia and their older son, Joe.

Next to the shop is the cheerful red barn where the Lacinas and the Coons (Alesia's sister and brother-in-law) began making Wildwood Harvest tofu; inside, the machines are a bright stainless steel and the rooms are clean and orderly. Outside, fields of soybean plants surround the farmstead, stretching north, east, and south over gently rolling land. You sense that if you walked into the Lacina's kitchen, it would be brightly lit, full of finished wood and colorful cabinets, and smelling of ginger, garlic, soy sauce, and, of course, tofu.

Wildwood Harvest Foods (until recently Midwest Harvest Corporation) is an organic soy foods company based in both Grinnell, Iowa, and Watsonville, California. Tom Lacina, president (and founder of Midwest Harvest), is a contemporary Renaissance man. A criminal defense attorney by training and experience, he is also a musician, a community theatre actor and director, and a farmer of the land that has been in his family for eighty years. His wife, Alesia—an artist by training—works as the company's graphic designer. Along with their sister and brother-in-law, Francene and Dave Coons, they were the brains and the brawn behind the launch of Wildwood Harvest Foods, a company that is environmentally sound, health-conscious, and whose product is an artistic creation.

But the aesthetics of tofu, you might ask? Isn't that an oxymoron? Tom would beg to differ. "Food at its best is one of our ultimate aesthetics," Tom says, in a conference room at the company's new building in Grinnell. "We look forward to eating dinner at the end of the day because it's a social and aesthetic experience." Tom believes that tofu can be the centerpiece of that experience. It's versatile—a flavor-carrier that adapts easily to whatever dish it's cooked in—and it's a healthy alternative to the traditional midwestern high-fat, high-starch fare. Not only that, but it adds value to a crop that's grown abundantly in Iowa, providing farmers with an alternative to the commodity-driven market.

Tom came to tofu making in a somewhat roundabout way. He grew up in Grinnell (his father is a retired farmer, still working in his shop at the age of ninety-one), but left home for the University of Iowa, where he eventually got both a law degree and a master's degree in urban and regional planning with an environmental emphasis. He began his law career working as a clerk for the Iowa Supreme Court. But in 1986, Tom and Alesia decided they wanted to move back to Grinnell. "The farm had a place in my heart," says Tom. "And I wanted our sons to be near their grandparents."

Tom did not get into tofu making right away. For fourteen years, he worked locally as an attorney while farming the family land (and in fact, he still maintains "counsel" status at his firm). But he knew that becoming yet another farmer trying to make it in Iowa's commodity-driven market was not an economical or even realistic plan. He and Alesia, along with Francene and Dave, decided to add value to their soybean crop by making tofu. They hoped the idea would enable them to both make a living and also bring a new healthy food to midwestern diets.

The farm began transitioning to organic in 1998, and in January of 1999 Midwest Harvest came out with their first product. Initially, Blooming Prairie, a natural food distributor based in the Midwest, picked up their tofu, and eventually they were able to sell it in local commercial grocery stores like Fareway and Hy-Vee. It was not easy at first. People weren't exactly enthusiastic about the product. "We've had to do a lot of missionary marketing," says Tom. "Out here, tofu is almost a joke. Everyone kids about it, and it gets a bad rap."

Of course, there's nothing new about tofu. It's already a staple in Asia. But bringing it successfully to the American Midwest was a challenge. "We're a salt-and-pepper society," Tom says. "Most of our flavor comes from fat and sugar. In traditional tofu-eating societies, spices are central."

Enter the Soy Sisters, Alesia and Francene. They've logged many hours in the Soy Sisters kitchen, finding new ways to use tofu as a staple at every meal. They've put together *A Tofu Cookbook* with almost fifty different recipes, from Artichoke Dip to Ultimate Tofu Cheesecake. Their recipes, presentations, and demonstrations have gone a long way toward making their tofu marketable in the Midwest. "We can stand in the grocery store and offer tastes of our tofu, and people are skeptical," says Tom. "But once we put a piece of smoked or braised tofu in their mouth, they're surprised."

Still, Midwest Harvest was a fledgling company, and Tom was having to work full time at his law firm in order to make ends meet. On a whim, he sent an email to Billy Bramblett, one of the founders of Wildwood Natural Foods, an organic soy foods company based in California. "I wrote him a note saying, 'I just started this tofu company. Any ideas?' and he wrote back, all excited." It turns out that Wildwood had been trying to partner with midwestern farmers to supply them with soybeans, but hadn't yet had any luck. After finding support from the Iowa Farm Bureau and tecTerra™ Food Capital Fund, Midwest Harvest and Wildwood Natural Foods merged to become Wildwood Harvest Foods.

The newly merged company offers a variety of soy food products, including soy milk, soy yogurt, soy smoothies, smoked and braised tofu, veggie burgers, tofu cutlets, and Bratos (a sausage made from a pork-tofu blend). The new plant in Grinnell—about five minutes from the Lacina farm—is dedicated to making soy dairy products. Changes have occurred, and the farm's tofu facility has found a new use as a full-fledged art studio. The sisters continue their old tricks in the kitchen, though both Dave and Francene have chosen to pursue new careers. Though the company is growing, they are still dedicated to organic, environmentally sound food production. And Tom and Alesia are still very much aware of the beauty of their farm, their family, and of a truly well-made cake of tofu.

UNSOUR GRAPES
Iowa's Emerging Wine Industry

Jean Gerrath thinks wine grapes and racehorses may have
more in common than most people realize. Jean, a develop-
mental plant biologist at the University of Northern Iowa, is
also president of the Iowa Grape Growers Association, whose
more than two hundred members want to restore both wine
and table-grape growing to the prominent and profitable place
it once enjoyed in Iowa agriculture. She sees horses and grapes
this way: "Grape growers and thoroughbred horse breeders
alike are passionate about what they do. They combine
intensity with enormous patience and an awful lot of curiosity.
Each vine, like each colt, has to be individually watched and
tended for years," she says. "And always, there's the mystery
of what will finally come out of the barrel or the starting gate."
In the end, the odds of vinting a great wine aren't much better
than of running a colt in the Kentucky Derby, but that only
seems to intensify the desire to try. "All too often," Jean
laughs, "enthusiasm outstrips common sense."

But common sense or not, Iowa's two hundred commercial grape
growers are working hard and betting they'll produce a winner.
A sense of history is on their side. For one thing, before the
right-jab-left-hook combination of Prohibition and 2,4-D
herbicides knocked it flat, Iowa's grape industry ranked sixth
among the states. Now, as fifty years ago, a big part of Iowa's
potential market is in wine grapes. At least six modern, winter-
hardy varieties that produce abundant and flavorful fruit are

under cultivation, and if prices hold steady, growers can expect to earn from three to five thousand dollars per acre for wine grapes at harvest.

"Expect" is a key term because grapevines typically take five years to yield a marketable crop, with three or four more years beyond that to reach full profitability. They are also a labor-intensive crop requiring as much as a hundred hours of attention per acre per year. Add in their vulnerability to adverse weather, and some growers look toward maximizing their return-per-acre. "Their answer," says Jean, "comes down to two words: wine and tourism. Wine is THE value-added agricultural product."

Grower Paul Tabor of Baldwin is one of the leaders of Iowa's vintner vanguard. He's tapping new resources such as United States Department of

Agriculture (USDA) Rural Development grants to train workers who will be key to viticulture expansion. In a first-of-its-kind effort, Paul matched $16,000 in USDA grant funds and hired recent University of Dubuque graduate Lucas McIntire as his apprentice wine maker. "Lucas took over all our wine making this year and enabled us to do two new wines. That let me focus on expanding production and marketing," Paul says.

Under USDA rules, if Lucas works in Iowa four years after completing his fifteen-month apprenticeship, the thirty-three thousand dollar cost of his training will be forgiven. He will take over as head wine maker at the Park Farm Winery west of Dubuque, with Paul Tabor's blessing. "Iowa needs more wine makers," Paul maintains. "Wine making in a lovely, bucolic setting is romance." And easy access to romance means tourism. However, "Unless

you're near a major population center," he says, "just one or two wineries won't pull in enough retail trade and overnight guests for you to make a go of it. But if you can get several good producers in your area, you can market wine trails where tourists will spend two or three days sampling wines, going to festivals and events, and so on. We need more skilled workers like Lucas building up our industry to make that happen."

From his vineyard atop one of the highest ridges in the Des Moines Valley region, Indianola's Ron Mark offers a sweeping view of a good life that wine makers and a thousand visitors a week can celebrate. His Somerset Winery's ledger says he sold sixty thousand bottles of wine last year with 2003 sales likely to rise to near ninety thousand, but what he's really selling, Ron says, "is a feeling of the good life I had in Italy."

Ron has been fascinated with wine making ever since his high school days. He explains, "I discovered you could add yeast to mom's grape juice, wait awhile, and bingo! You've got wine!" But it was during the five years he was stationed with the Army in Italy, spending as much time as possible with a wine-making farm family, that he found his vision of what living well is all about. "My adopted family and their friends, working together, bringing good things out of the earth with their own hands, celebrating the cycle of the seasons, eating, drinking, singing, laughing, dancing—living simply and joyfully and gratefully—that is living well!"

Ron carried his memories and vision through a globe-hopping career doing electronics work with the Federal Aviation Administration, but finally "I said to my wife, 'I've just gotta make wine. It's more rewarding than anything else I've ever done.'" His quest for a place to live his dream ended in 1989 when he planted his first vines in Warren County, "a fifteen-minute drive from where I grew up," he says.

Now Ron has twelve-and-a-half acres in vines, and he buys grapes from five other local vineyards. His Somerset Winery produces twelve kinds of red and white wine from ten different varieties of pre-dominantly French-bred, disease-resistant, winter hardy hybrids—Marechal Foch, St. Vincent, Seyval Blanc, Frontenac, Cynthiana. Somerset's full-time staff consists of himself, an apprentice, a production manager, a bookkeeper, and a part-time events coordinator—hardly enough to cultivate the vines, harvest, vinify, and market an anticipated 86,000 bottles in 2003.

To make up the labor shortage, Ron applies his "Italian way." Every Saturday morning during the fall, Ron counts on thirty-five to forty volunteer "harvest helpers" to show up to pick grapes and take them to the press—or climb in a vat and stomp 'em, just the way we did back in Italy. After that," he says, "the rest of the day is a festival. We have lunch out on the terrace, wine, some of the best live music in Iowa, and dancing."

Volunteers get a discount on wine they buy, but anybody can come for the party. "We'll rack up a thousand dollars a day or better in sales, and that feeds the demand in the local retail and restaurant markets," Ron says. "We've got a network of sixteen retail shops in the local area, and we don't even try to sell outside central Iowa. Right now our steady customers, our good friends, will buy up our whole vintage within four or five months after we release it."

Ron sees a solid prospect of selling 200,000 bottle vintages in a few years, and he believes many others will share his success. "Iowa has a reputation as a place where you can get away from the rat race and still taste the good life. And it's true: Iowa is a great place to live. Well, one of these days people may say, 'Ah, Iowa: peaceful little towns, friendly people, and those lovely, full-bodied Foch wines ....'"

ENVISIONING A NEW AGRARIAN LANDSCAPE
Southeast Iowa Nut Growers Association

The rolling farm fields of southeast Iowa may seem an unlikely site to begin a revolution, but a small group of landowners between the Mississippi and the Des Moines river valleys are pursuing a dream they hope will radically change the rural Iowa landscape and boost sustainable agriculture throughout the nation for generations.

The revolution actually started ten years ago when several landowners began growing hybrid Chinese chestnut trees. While working for the Louisa County Conservation Board, Tom Wahl, a forty-three-year-old from Wapello, spearheaded the effort. The board had recently purchased an eleven-hundred-acre complex of agricultural fields, backwater sloughs, and timber along the Iowa River, north of Wapello. Tom was looking for vegetation that could be planted in the area for habitat and other purposes.

"I was trying to find polycultures of perennials," he says. Using perennials, he hoped to develop a holistic land management system for the conservation area. A species that caught his eye was the hybrid chestnut. So, collaborating with the Michigan-based Chestnut Alliance, he introduced the trees to private landowners through a public seminar. More than eighty individuals attended the meeting. Several subsequently planted trees on their land, and ten years later those trees are giving these perennial pioneers hope for the future.

"I see chestnuts as where soybeans were fifty or sixty years ago," says John Wittrig, a chestnut grower from Winfield. John thinks the same changes in attitude and business acumen that eventually boosted soybean production will affect chestnut production. To help make that happen, around twenty-five growers have informally organized as the Southeast Iowa Nut Growers Association. "We think woody agriculture will be one of the solutions for rural Iowa," John explains. A retired psychologist, John and his wife, Betty, planted three hundred of the nut trees on a three-acre city lot in 1993.

In 1999 their chestnut trees produced 50 pounds of nuts—their first commercial harvest. That number jumped to 400 pounds the next year before falling back to 250 pounds in 2001. A two-year cycle of high production followed by low production is normal for nut trees. John and Betty harvest their crop by picking up fallen nuts by hand. However, growers can use customized mechanical equipment similar to machines that pick up golf balls and specialized, hand-operated machines that resemble old push lawnmowers.

The Wittrigs were certified as organic growers in 2001 and received four dollars per pound for their crop in 2002. Chestnuts not certified as organically grown fetched two dollars a pound in the same year. Tom Wahl expects that when the area's chestnut groves mature in another ten years, the income potential will be substantial. "I think four thousand to six thousand dollars per acre would be pretty reasonable," he suggests.

For John, that potential income, combined with the small annual overhead and maintenance costs associated with chestnut production, makes an ideal combination. "I didn't have any expense for seed and only had to mow the planting twice this year," he explains. Income, however, is not the only reason the Wittrigs made the decision to switch from traditional row crops to woody agriculture. "Growing chestnuts seemed like a project that had a good promise of saving the land and being sustainable," John says.

The Wittrigs have already seen benefits to the land. When they first planted the trees, the land was so compacted after being in row crops that they had a difficult time digging the holes for the containerized stock. "It was like concrete," John says. They finally got all the trees planted, mulched them with wood chips, and seeded between the rows with a mixture of timothy and clover.

A few years later, when they needed to go back to replant a few of the trees, they discovered a dramatic difference. The rock-hard, parking lot surface they had struggled to open earlier had been replaced by a loose, easily turned blanket of soil that came up by the spadeful. "The benefits to the soil have been amazing," observes John. "The soil tilth has changed and improved so much in only a couple of years."

Bill Brookhieser readily agrees. The lead mechanic for the Burlington Community School District, Bill and his wife, Connie, are growing nine acres of chestnut trees on a twenty-acre farmstead near Wever. Enjoying the reaction of his neighbors, Bill reports, "I live in a housing development, and the road goes right by the trees. The neighbors think it's great."

The Brookhiesers gathered about six hundred pounds of nuts last year from the three acres of trees that are currently producing. Like the Wittrigs, they are also becoming certified organic growers. Bill is planning to use the trees as a source of retirement income, but he also wants to leave a legacy for his children.

"My dad and uncle and grandpa started a trucking business years ago and built it up," he says, explaining how he grew up working in the family business. It was an experience he hopes his children can repeat. "I wanted to start something up and get my kids involved in it."

That attitude is what gives chestnut production a good chance to succeed, points out Dan Dolan, a grower from Muscatine. Dan and his wife, Celeste, are so convinced chestnuts have a solid future, they've planted twenty-eight acres in trees and are making plans to add another thirty-five acres. The couple owns more than two hundred acres of land that is either in the federal Conservation Reserve Program (CRP) or part of their tree farm. Dan acknowledges his regular job as a builder and developer has given him more flexibility with his ground, but says the opportunity and need is there for other landowners.

"Row crop production is the mainstay of Iowa, but commodity prices have fallen, not risen. Agricultural production needs to diversify, but it's got to be reality based," Dan explains. He believes that chestnuts, historically a food staple, are a perfect mixture of protein and carbohydrate and offer that reality, but he agrees there is a risk to planting large acreages to trees. "We're just on the leading edge, and either I'm really smart or I'm really stupid and time will tell," he explains. "But," he goes on to ask, "if people aren't willing to take a risk, how can it work?"

Tom Wahl also believes chestnut production will be successful in the United States because the country currently imports about forty million pounds of chestnuts annually. The nuts can be used in a variety of ways. In addition to being eaten raw, they can be frozen, pureed, sliced, and ground into flour. A University of Nebraska researcher has developed a machine that steam peels and vacuum packs chestnuts, paving the way for increased distribution and storage options. Most of the southeast Iowa crop is sold to area ethnic groups, especially Asian communities, but Tom expects this to change as growers continue to expand.

"Almost all chestnuts available in this country come from Europe or Korea, and they tend to be low quality," he says. "It may be years before U.S. production can even meet the demand."

Tom and his wife, Kathy, have devoted seven acres of their fifty-five-acre Red Fern Farm to agroforestry production. They are purchasing another thirty-one acres to expand those plantings. While chestnuts have been an important part of that effort, the couple is also looking at kiwi, pawpaw, persimmon, and several other woody species.

"I'm interested in woody crops that can be grown without a lot of labor or chemical input," Tom says. That may seem a radical departure from tradition, but for the Southeast Iowa Nut Growers, it's just a step into the future.

Iowa Ingenuity at Work

Essay by John A. Schillinger

What does the future hold for Iowa agriculture? If the events of the past one hundred years can be put into a word, it would be *change*. In 1903, my grandfather used a team of horses to plow the sandy soil of Anne Arundel County, Maryland, and planted tobacco. In 2003, most Maryland tobacco farmers have taken advantage of the state tobacco buy-out program and are scrambling to find other crops for their acres. My brother still has the red Farmall tractor my father purchased over fifty years ago, but he uses the newer John Deere when he plants tomatoes, green beans, and squash for marketing right from the family farm or for delivery to local chain grocery stores. *Change* is never easy. It might involve generational differences of opinion or learning how to do new things; it always involves risk. But to those who love the land and love the way of life farming provides, the risk is worth the pursuit—of an idea, of a dream, of a goal.

In the past half-century, Iowa farmers have typically grown corn and beans and raised hogs and cattle. The size of farms has increased, and technology is marketed prominently through the seed sown on those farms. Economics and politics are an integral part of the agriculture picture. How can farmers compete—earn a profit for their labor—with rising land and production costs, unpredictable market prices, and increasing foreign competition for corn and soybean markets? The people whose stories were featured in this chapter are examples of American ingenuity at work. There are essential characteristics they all share.

First, they know their business. They are good managers. They search out industry trends and demographic patterns. They recognize problems and search out solutions. Second, they cultivate relationships with trusted people—family, friends, and experts—who lend support, encouragement, and wisdom when the going gets tough. Third, they listen to their customers. Gaining product acceptance and building consumer loyalty in an entry-level, niche market is the prelude to expansion. And fourth, they are realistic enough to know that whatever the dream, it's going to take more time than they planned on, more effort than they supposed, and more money than they banked on.

An example of an entrepreneurial spirit is Steve Demos, the founder of White Wave™, the company that introduced Silk® Soymilk in 1996 in refrigerated store cases. Why would anyone pay more than twice the price of dairy milk for a soy product that had been on store shelves in Tetra Paks™ for years? Demos wagered on what looked like a rising trend among consumers: concern for health and wellness and "natural" foods. When the Food and Drug Administration and the American Heart Association agreed in 1999 that "twenty-five grams of soy protein a day, when consumed as part of a diet low in saturated fat and cholesterol, may reduce the risk of heart disease," people soon realized that Silk® Soymilk would be a very easy way to get all the goodness of (organic) soy into their diets. White Wave today employs over one hundred people and has annual sales nearing $140 million.

Closer to my heart is my boyhood friend and college roommate, Lambert "Lem" Cissel. While still in school, Lem worked nights at the USDA and bought a truck on credit. He planted grass seed on land he rented on the edge of one of the fastest developing suburban areas in the country. All those developers needed sodded lawns to help sell their houses—and Lem delivered. The business grew, and Lem branched out to growing trees. The problem soon became evident: how could he guarantee the tree to grow and not go broke if the buyer didn't water it? His solution was "the bag." I saw many prototypes in Lem's basement and even tested one in my own yard. It wasn't easy—materials, design, testing, patenting, production—and, oh yes, the marketing. You can imagine my delight last summer when, while driving through the new Des Moines Water Works facility at Maffitt Lake, I counted seventy-two Treegators® around the newly planted crabapple trees.

Renewing Iowa's countryside is a challenge, and it most likely is going to involve change. Not everyone wants to move to the city. For people to remain in rural Iowa there has to be a way for them to earn a living. As I travel this state, I am impressed with the entrepreneurs among us who are providing jobs: people who are milling soybeans into flour and others who are making tofu in Grinnell; farmers who are extracting oil from soybeans in Cherokee; three women whose fondness for goats led to developing a cheese factory near Woodward. I also know first hand of the gaps in the value-added chain. My company has to truck soybeans through three states to achieve the precise processing and milling needed for one customer. Why can't we do that right here? Well, there's a problem —and if this is Iowa, there's someone out there who has a solution.

John A. Schillinger lives in Cumming, Iowa, and has thirty-six years of experience in plant breeding. After retiring from Asgrow in 1999, he established Schillinger Seed, Inc., to develop food-grade soybeans, and Heartland Fields, LLC.

CHAPTER SIX
Energy

The boilers of the Alliant Energy Company, which powers Iowa's Chariton Valley, will burn either coal or switchgrass. Since switchgrass costs three times as much as coal, simple logic would dictate choosing coal for fuel. But the logic of energy costs has grown more sophisticated in recent years. While coal is currently the cheaper, simpler economic solution, in the long run its social and environmental costs may outrun the short-run advantages. And so today a percentage of the fuel burned in Alliant Energy's power plant is switchgrass.

There is an awareness now in the Chariton Valley—and in Spirit Lake, Waverly, Ralston, and elsewhere in Iowa—that the environmental impacts associated with fossil-fuels and nuclear energy can no longer be ignored. What also cannot be ignored are the consequences of our dependence on foreign oil. Home-grown, renewable energy is good for the environment and for Iowa's economy. The stories in this chapter explore how visionary Iowans are creating new sources of energy. And in the case of the Iowa Association of Municipal Utilities, how they have set an example for the practical use of renewable energy in the design of their new building in Ankeny.

HARVESTING THE WIND
Waverly Light and Power and Spirit Lake School District

A familiar sight on the Iowa landscape each autumn are the tractors that comb the earth, harvesting thousands of acres of corn and soybeans each year. Less familiar to many are the statuesque structures dotting the horizon, harvesting one of the state's newest crops: the wind. Wind energy might be a new crop on the scene, but it has been nonetheless eagerly adopted. Iowa now boasts approximately four hundred utility-scale wind turbines.

Take Waverly. When the town's community leaders first began exploring wind power, they were told it just wouldn't work. "The energy experts told us our winter was too severe, our thunderstorms were too violent, and our wind patterns didn't meet electric load profiles," says Glenn Cannon, general manager of Waverly Light and Power. "We weren't convinced."

In 1993, Waverly became the first community west of the Mississippi to add wind to its energy portfolio. Today, its three turbines serve the yearly electrical needs of 761 homes and supply 5 percent of the annual energy provided by the power company, one of the highest rates in the world.

"When I stand under the 'Skeets 4,' I get goosebumps," says Kelly Vowels, the power company's marketing specialist. In the center of the Norma and Russell "Skeets" Walther farmstead, surrounded by cornfields, is Skeets 4, the community's largest turbine. And indeed, the knowledge that the gently swishing giant windmill is producing clean, renewable energy for Waverly families brings a goodwill goosebump or two. The turbine's 85-foot blades sit on top of a 231-foot tower and sweep an area nearly half the size of a football field. Using the wind's power offsets nearly 8,850 tons of carbon dioxide, a leading greenhouse gas associated with climate change.

The success of the turbine is due to its size, particularly the height of the tower. There is nothing mysterious about wind collection, says Glenn. "There has been a huge improvement in wind generation technology, and we were brave enough to try it. We took the mystery out of it."

But part of the community's success has something to do with commodities a little more intangible than technology: pride, ownership, and vision. It is significant that Waverly's turbines are all named "Skeets," a tribute to Skeets Walther, who died in the summer of 2002. Skeets, like the many community members he represents, was committed to clean, renewable energy. The importance of community pride is summarized by Patti Cale-Finnegan, energy services coordinator for the Iowa Association of Municipal Utilities. "Leaders who promote wind energy understand that we're coming to

ENERGY

a change in the way we produce electricity, and they want to be on board," Patti says. "They see their investment in wind energy as a kind of legacy—something they can do that will live on for the future of the community."

Waverly Light and Power is tapping this reservoir of environmental goodwill not only in Waverly, but worldwide. A program they have dubbed "Green Tags" makes it possible to donate to the community's wind technology by purchasing tax deductible "green tag" certificates that guarantee that wind power or another renewable energy is substituted for traditional power. The power company received a national award in the summer of 2002 for its innovative program—the first of its kind in the nation.

But towns are not the only pioneers on the wind power trail. In Spirit Lake, the idea for harnessing the wind's power came to the former superintendent of schools and the school board president one cold fall afternoon in early 1991 when they were attending a flag football game. As always, the wind howled around them. Spirit Lake, they concluded, was one windy city. Unlike Waverly, whose natural geography is not particularly well suited for wind, Spirit Lake is a magnificent wind catcher. The community sits atop a ridge on the geological divide between the Mississippi and Missouri river valleys, and the wind blows an average of fourteen miles per hour, daily.

In 1993, the Spirit Lake School District installed its first wind turbine, which quickly provided 100 percent of the electricity used by the elementary school. That turbine has since completely paid for itself. In fall 2001, the district installed a second, much larger turbine that provides for the balance of the district's energy needs, including powering the middle school, high school, and athletic fields. Today, Spirit Lake has the distinction of being the first school system in the nation to provide 100 percent of its energy from wind. Together, the turbines offset approximately $135,000 in energy costs each year. Superintendent Tim Grieves estimates that the district will pay back the loan for the second turbine by July 2008. After that, every dollar saved can be invested in education.

The wind turbines at Spirit Lake do more than generate electricity; they also generate a unique opportunity for learning. Teachers in the school district incorporate the system's environmently-friendly energy source in their curricula. Kindergarteners and high-school seniors alike understand that wind energy—in contrast to fossil fuels—produces no harmful byproducts. As students learn about global warming, air pollution, and nuclear byproducts, they increasingly value the energy that powers their schools.

FARMERS FUELING ENERGY INDEPENDENCE

West Central Cooperative

Visible for miles across the prairie, the new biodiesel plant at West Central Cooperative in Ralston stands as a monument to the power of the bean.

Biodiesel is a fuel made entirely from natural oil—most commonly soybean oil. A clean-burning fuel, which also serves as an engine cleaner and lubricant, biodiesel can be mixed with petroleum or used by itself. According to Myron Danzer, sales and production project manager for West Central Soy, "It's a product whose time has come."

Soy biodiesel is the hottest thing since ethanol, and West Central has built one of the largest biodiesel plants in the world. At a cost of twelve million dollars, the state's third largest farmer-owned co-op replaced an earlier and much smaller biodiesel batch plant. The new plant, when operating at full capacity, will produce twelve million gallons of biodiesel a year.

Soy biodiesel has benefits for farmers, communities, and the environment. Unlike petroleum-based diesel that is currently used to fuel most trucks, tractors, and school buses, soy biodiesel does not release harmful chemicals into the atmosphere. Soy biodiesel relies on a home-grown, renewable product, not on foreign, nonrenewable fossil fuels. Because of these benefits, federal legislation has been passed to help increase the production and use of biodiesel.

"The 2002 federal energy bill contains a tax incentive for people who use biodiesel," Myron notes. "And the 2002 farm bill includes a program to make the fuel competitive with petroleum." The Environmental Protection Agency is also entering the picture. It has called for a 97 percent reduction in sulfur levels in most on-road diesel fuel by 2006. Sulfur, currently added to petroleum-based diesel fuel as a lubricant to protect engines, is a toxic pollutant.

"Biodiesel can replace that lubricant," says Myron. "You can't argue with its value." The National Biodiesel Board reports that a 2 percent soy biodiesel blend (that is 98 percent petroleum-based diesel plus 2 percent biodiesel) increases lubricity by 66 percent. Myron adds that biodiesel has undergone stringent health and safety testing by the Environmental Protection Agency and passed with flying colors. "They couldn't put enough biodiesel in the cage to kill a rat," he reports.

With a powerful promotion entity behind it in the National Biodiesel Board, and consumption of biodiesel jumping from five million gallons in 2000 to a projected twenty-five million gallons in 2002, it appears the market can head nowhere but up. Thirty-three state legislatures are currently considering bills promoting the production and use of biodiesel—spurred on, no doubt, by a renewed deter-mination to lessen America's dependence on foreign oil.

So although West Central Soy was the world's largest biodiesel production facility at the time of its opening in August 2002, they do not expect that record to stand for long. Other investors will jump on the biodiesel bandwagon, and in anticipation of that, West Central has formed a company called Renewable Energy Group to provide such clients with technical assistance and marketing. "First we value-added the soybeans," says Myron, "now we're value-adding our knowledge."

Although it is the newest, biodiesel is far from the only soy product to come out of West Central Cooperative. In addition to marketing 65 million bushels of grain a year for its 3,500 members, it also annually processes nearly 176 million bushels of seed beans, 130,000 tons of feed, 8 million bushels of soybeans, and 72 million pounds of soy oil into methyl esters and biodiesel. Glycerin, which is a byproduct of the biodiesel process, is sold to industrial manufacturers to be used in hundreds of products from makeup to toothpaste.

Another important product of the plant's biodiesel process is soybean meal. Because West Central uses a pressing process rather than a chemical process to separate meal from oil, the resulting meal can be turned into premium livestock feed. Myron says West Central's meal, sold as SoyPlus, is fed to dairy cattle worldwide. West Central is the largest supplier in the world in the "bypass protein market"—which means that dairy cows can digest the feed better and receive more benefit from it.

The biodiesel plant itself is a metallic labyrinth of pipes, tubes, and machines. But the whole configuration is so streamlined, and the operation so computerized, that one employee can run it. "We are the most technologically advanced biodiesel plant around," says Myron, tracing a finger across a computer screen that monitors tanks and pipes.

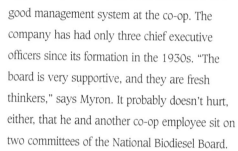

Myron attributes West Central's aggressive position in the biodiesel market to a good management system at the co-op. The company has had only three chief executive officers since its formation in the 1930s. "The board is very supportive, and they are fresh thinkers," says Myron. It probably doesn't hurt, either, that he and another co-op employee sit on two committees of the National Biodiesel Board.

The biodiesel manufacturing process that West Central uses, and will assist other companies in acquiring, was itself a byproduct of its production of methyl esters. The co-op has produced methyl esters from soybean oil for years, and in the process, developed a way of purifying that product into biodiesel. "That's what we developed," says Myron. "This plant is a result of that research and development, trial and error, and the school of hard knocks."

Myron is proud of the economic impact the plant has had, and will continue to have, on the surrounding west central Iowa community. Many of the co-op's 222 employees were area farm kids, including Myron himself, who started working nights at West Central's feed mill in 1985. "There's no doubt this plant helps rural development in our area. All the companies involved in construction are Iowa companies, and now we have hired extra people to help with Renewable Energy Group."

FIELDS OF ENERGY
Chariton Valley Biomass Project

In Chuck McCarty's vision for southern Iowa, residents would value their local natural resources and use them responsibly to build their economies and communities. Chuck started the Chariton Valley Resource Conservation and Development (RC&D) in the early 1980s with this vision in mind. After he passed away in 1992, the RC&D continued to pursue his dream of enlightened land use and innovation, sponsoring projects from elk and walleye production to better use of forages, farm ponds, and forest resources. But the best known of these efforts is the Chariton Valley Biomass Project, where switchgrass is being used to generate electricity.

Today, a thriving partnership between farmers and Alliant Energy is making renewable energy production a very real opportunity in southern Iowa. Prairie Lands Bio-Products is a cooperative of nearly seventy local farmers who can see beyond corn and soybeans. "Members of Prairie Lands, like most southern Iowa farmers, don't want to raise crops on the area's rolling lands," says John Sellers, president of Prairie Lands and member of the Iowa State Soil Conservation Committee. The combination of government price supports and the need to feed families and send kids to college gives the farmers little choice aside from commodity crops. Yet, John says they would prefer a sustainable alternative. "Most of these folks welcome the opportunity to help build a sustainable market for a crop that is better for the soil and one that they can all easily raise," he explains.

And raise they have; these farmers have planted nearly six thousand acres of land in the Conservation Reserve Program (CRP) and other lands in energy-generating switchgrass in south central Iowa. Switchgrass, a plant native to southern Iowa, does an outstanding job of retaining the soil, filtering the water, and replacing lost carbon in the soil. This is extremely important in southern Iowa where soils are more erosive and fragile than in the rest of the state.

As with most projects that seek to develop alternative crops, finding a market for the switchgrass was the biggest limiting factor. Pound for pound, switchgrass and most other biomass products come close to equaling the Btu value of coal, but at first glance the economics seem to foil an otherwise perfect match for southern Iowa farms. Switchgrass production costs are similar to those of other forage crops, but are almost three times the delivered cost of coal from Wyoming.

So what makes the project work? In part, a better financial accounting system that values nontraditional costs and benefits when evaluating agriculture and energy markets. The protection of soil, water, and air has economic value, and these ecological services can prevent significant public costs now and in the future. Long-term use of fossil fuels, such as coal, involves additional costs to the public that currently are not added to the price of the fuel. (Air quality problems and the impacts of global warming are two prime examples of unrecovered energy costs.) When all the costs and benefits are considered, biomass becomes more attractive as a renewable energy source.

Alliant Energy recognized the long-term potential of biomass as well as the increasing value of environmental benefits. Using cost-share assistance from the Department of Energy as well as significant resources of its own, Alliant Energy has modified what some would say is its flagship power plant so that it can burn switchgrass along with its usual fuel.

The modifications themselves sprang from a sound partnership between agriculture and energy production. While engineers designed the modifications to put switchgrass into the boiler, it took farmers with forage handling experience to make it work. Gary Kelderman of Kelderman Manufacturing and his crew worked countless hours to get the right consistency of ground biomass to flow through the pneumatic system to reach the boiler for a successful burn.

The modifications will allow 5 percent of the Alliant Energy power plant's fuel to come from switchgrass. It sounds like a small amount until you realize that the facility is so large that it will take 200,000 tons of grass grown on 50,000 acres of land to meet the 5 percent goal. Ironically, that's about how much CRP land is in the watershed above Lake Rathbun, which goes to show that biomass could protect the lake long after the CRP program ends. This has enormous environmental potential when you consider that most of southern Iowa gets its water from Rathbun Regional Water Association, which in turn draws its water from the discharge of Lake Rathbun.

The premise of the biomass project is fairly simple: native grasses are potentially valuable sources of fuel and fiber because of their high Btu value relative to coal. Yet they produce fewer emissions, protect soil and water, and reduce carbon dioxide in the atmosphere. With biomass, farmers have an alternative crop that is environmentally friendly and easy to adopt. Not only does it grow well in southern Iowa, but it harvests just like hay. As a result, grassland alternatives are helping to break the hold of commodity programs in southern Iowa before Lake Rathbun and other water resources are damaged beyond repair.

Much of Iowa was once covered by native tallgrass prairie. It formed the soil. It held the water. Today, Iowa imports most of its energy while exporting much of what it produces on the land. With new technologies and increasing interest in domestic energy sources, the Chariton Valley project has established the model for innovative uses of native grasses such as fiber, bio-based petroleum substitutes, ethanol, and hydrogen. Returning to native grasses as a crop to replace petroleum is the perfect example of Chuck McCarty's vision for southern Iowa. Through programs like this, communities are recognizing the best use of their resources and creating a locally based economy that allows everyone to prosper.

A BETTER PLACE TO WORK
Iowa Association of Municipal Utilities

As the energy services coordinator for the Iowa Association of Municipal Utilities (IAMU), Patti Cale-Finnegan works on a variety of projects designed to help the association's members conserve energy. With a mission "to support and strengthen Iowa's municipal utilities," IAMU represents 550 cities with municipally owned gas, electric, water, and telecommunications utilities.

In an office and training complex that features a seventy-five-seat auditorium and a ten-acre training ground, IAMU provides education in establishing safe work environments, complying with OSHA standards, creating waste water systems, and even climbing those utility poles.

IAMU's work often requires staff to log long hours, holed up in their offices in the IAMU building in Ankeny. Although such an arrangement may make some people feel isolated, IAMU staff are literally surrounded by inspiration. The building, constructed in 1997, is an incredible example of cost-effective energy efficiency. A variety of technologies and design elements were incorporated into the training and office complex in order to reduce energy consumption by up to 45 percent of that used by a typical, code-compliant building.

As the sun passes over the complex, constructed on an east-west axis, its light slowly inches across the rows of offices and cubicles. Daylight is a precious commodity, and the building is designed to use it to its maximum capacity. White-painted interior surfaces reflect and diffuse the daylight, and high office windows allow the outside light easily to reach desks and workstations.

Sunlight isn't the only light source in the building—otherwise employees would find themselves working in the dark during the winter months. Electric lights supplement the daylight, but unlike typical lights, they don't simply burn brightly throughout the day, rather their levels rise and fall, according to the amount of daylight available. Stationed above Patti's desk is a photosensor, which monitors the light levels. "It detects the amount of natural light and brightens or dims the artificial light," explains Patti. "It constantly works to maintain a balance." Patti and her co-workers are oblivious to the extremely subtle level-changes made by the lights.

In addition to saving money and conserving energy, this lighting system is also intended to support IAMU's most important resource: its people. "Natural light helps to promote the productivity, comfort, and good feelings of workers," says Patti with a smile. "It also provides a connection with the outdoors."

In addition to the sun's lighting, the complex also allows the outdoor breezes to rustle the paperwork adorning the desks. "We can actually open our windows. It was one of our requests when we worked on the building's design," laughs Patti. "That would typically drive an engineer crazy, but it works."

But IAMU's employees don't have to depend upon opening windows or dressing in layers to keep cool in the summer or warm in the winter. The IAMU complex employs a geothermal system that uses the natural (and constant) temperature of the earth to provide heat in the winter and cooling in the summer. A water/antifreeze solution circulates through more than two miles of piping that is installed in 33 wells that drop 175 feet into the ground.

"The earth's temperature is usually about fifty degrees Fahrenheit," explains Patti. "The pipes tap into wells that are located just north of the building. As the solution travels back here, it brings in the heat from the warm earth in the winter and, in the summer, takes the heat from the building and discharges it back into the ground." Eight four-ton pumps distribute warm or cool air throughout the building. "We don't use supplemental heat," says Patti. And her office showed no evidence of extra sweaters or desk fans.

Although the geothermal unit's cost was higher than a typical system, its long-term savings is also high. The system provides energy savings of 40 percent over other heat and air conditioning equipment. And once that cool or warm air reaches the building, it is there to stay. With the use of the Icynene Insulation System, the building is airtight. The insulation material was sprayed between the wall studs, expanding and sealing any cracks, gaps, or holes. "The first winter we were in the building, it was very cold," says Patti, "but for the months of December and January, the electric bill for the entire complex, including heat, lighting, running computers, everything, was only $1,022."

By the time the IAMU staff's work day is done, the sunlight may have clocked out hours ago. The complex's outdoor lighting, although designed to save energy by powering down during typical nonworking hours, doesn't compromise anyone's safety. Driveway and parking lot light fixtures are set for 150 watts until 10 p.m. At that time, those lights drop to 50 watts. Employees can "power up" the lights with manual switches, but the fixtures are also equipped with motion sensors.

Additionally, the lights are designed to illuminate the ground and not the sky. "They're sight lights, not night lights," laughs Patti. Instead of typical direct lights, which beam overhead, the IAMU's outdoor light fixtures are down-lights, shining light down upon the ground—allowing employees to both find their cars and see the starry sky above.

Back in her office on this sunny Iowa afternoon, Patti says the budget for the airtight complex was just as tight. "We are a training center for our member municipalities, and we wanted to serve as an example of innovative technologies. But nothing we did was experimental," says Patti. "Everything was a proven science or technique. We couldn't afford for something not to work.

Everything needed to be integrated into one system." Each element was evaluated for a life-cycle cost analysis, in addition to the up-front costs.

And, if opening a window doesn't provide the proper outdoor-fix, Patti can escape the confines of her energy-conserving building and step out into the building's outdoor conservation efforts. Located near Carney Marsh, a forty-acre protected wetland, IAMU is surrounded by beautiful fields of prairie grasses and flowers that explode into hues of rich gold and brilliant purple. The prairie helps to control soil erosion and filter sediment. As construction of the building began, so did these conservation efforts. Temporary sediment basins, constructed wetlands, compost use, silt fences, and temporary and permanent seedings all contribute to keeping soil on the site and out of the marsh.

Patti pauses during her outdoor excursion to glance at the outdoor wireless, solar-powered weather station, positioned out in the prairie. "It's been wonderful to share our knowledge with our members and still be learning so much ourselves everyday," she offers. "There's something new everyday."

Energy Policy Transforming the Countryside

Essay by David Osterberg

OUR rich, midwestern land can make energy that does not saturate our atmosphere with extra greenhouse gasses. Some of us know that. In Minnesota, Wisconsin, and here in Iowa, state law requires that electric sellers derive a percentage of their power from renewable sources. These renewable energy requirements are important because they give wind power producers a market and provide a necessary incentive to build a biomass-to-electricity industry.

Farmers in Northern Europe gain from energy policies that give incentives to local power production. This didn't happen by chance. In Europe, leaders are committed to reducing greenhouse gasses. The European Union (EU) has signed the international treaty that requires they reduce greenhouse gases by 8 percent over the next ten years. The EU goal is to have 22 percent of electricity and 12 percent of all energy sources from renewable sources by the year 2010.

Knowing what Europe was doing and feeling that sharing their progress would lead to policy changes at home, five of us tried a novel idea. We decided to ride bikes through farm country in Germany and Denmark, writing about what we saw and sending digital pictures to our website, www.greenbike.org. As part of our preparation we visited with newspaper editors and other media people in Iowa to try to arrange press coverage. To make ourselves more news worthy, one of our bikes pulled a trailer with a solar panel. The panel could power our computer, recharge our camera battery, or run a small motor, which allowed the rider pulling the solar panel to get some power assist up hills.

We found that the state of Schleswig-Holstein in Germany already gets 18 percent of its electricity from the wind. We in Iowa currently get about 3 percent of our electricity from wind power. That is better than nothing, but state government does not currently have a goal to increase this amount.

Our bike tour visited a straw-burning plant at Sakskobing, Denmark, which produces electricity from wheat straw in an efficient "district-heating" operation that uses what in the U.S. would be waste heat. The heat produced is used for heating homes and businesses in two towns. The Sakskobing plant is uncommon because in addition to its efficiency benefits, it uses straw for fuel.

Wind generators and biomass-to-energy plants now produce 10 percent of Denmark's total energy. Danish wind turbine manufacturers dominate the industry worldwide. Energy policy is integrated with agricultural policy, and consequently farmers make money while the atmosphere receives less greenhouse gas.

During our three-week tour in June and July 2002, the "greenbike team" was covered by Iowa newspapers and radio. KUNI, the public station in Cedar Falls, Iowa, interviewed one of us each Wednesday morning from wherever we were on our travels. We presented renewable energy in a unique way that appealed to nearly everyone. A right-wing talk show host and I spent about five minutes of air time disagreeing strongly about global warming but then spent the next thirty minutes agreeing about how Danish energy policy was transforming the countryside and giving farmers a crop of renewable power to sell.

Our European tour led to a second solar bike trip—this time in Iowa. For three days we visited sites all over the state. In Forest City, we saw a high school that has its own wind turbine. From there, we rode to a large eighty-nine turbine wind farm near Joice. The next day we stopped at a dairy in Westgate that produces methane gas for a small on-farm power plant, and then we went on to Waverly Municipal Utility's small wind farm. In Nevada, we visited an Iowa State University research facility that is developing ways to use biomass for energy and as a substitute for petrochemicals. We finished our ride at the University of Iowa campus power plant that produces electricity and steam from a combination of coal and oat hulls. TV and radio stations and several newspapers covered the various segments of our tour. State legislators, a utility commissioner, many energy experts, and Iowa First Lady Christie Vilsack rode on various stages of the tour.

Will our solar bike tours help to change energy policy in our state? It is too early to tell. In 2003 Governor Vilsack recommended $50 million in incentives for small-scale wind projects and for biomass energy plants, but the legislature rejected the idea. The five members of our greenbike team continue to make presentations about what we learned in our travels. Talking about the tours is part of a legislative effort to increase the amount of renewable electricity that energy sellers in Iowa must produce or purchase. But significant progress in renewable-energy policy will continue only if citizens persist in demanding that Iowa legislators pass new laws. At the very least, we greenbikers think we have motivated more citizens to push the issue.

David Osterberg is associate clinical professor in the Department of Occupational and Environmental Health at the University of Iowa. He served twelve years in the Iowa General Assembly, where he chaired the House Committee on Energy and Environmental Protection and the Committee on Agriculture. Currently he is executive director of the Iowa Policy Project, a nonprofit Iowa think tank.

CHAPTER SEVEN
Community

Though many celebrate the rise of the virtual community, skeptics point out that electronic media cannot generate the cohesive ties that characterize stable communities of interdependent individuals and families. Others question whether cohesive communities are even possible in major population centers any more. In the anonymity of edge-city sprawl, neighbors co-exist without ever knowing one another.

By contrast, several of the stories in earlier chapters of this book have described the importance of establishing face-to-face contacts in local communities as a key component of renewing the countryside. This chapter explores that theme in greater depth, describing specific community projects designed to strengthen "the grid of human relationships," among them the ties between people in town and those in the country. There is a particular emphasis on projects that foster the mutual trust among neighbors that characterizes strong communities, for it is here, in the common sense of shared responsibility for community resources, that the countryside will find its most vigilant protectors.

BUILDING A COMMUNITY FOOD SYSTEM

University of Northern Iowa Local Food Project

The décor trumpets to customers at Rudy's Tacos in Waterloo that they are not in a same-old-same-old chain restaurant. Boisterously hued, Fifties-era Formica-topped, chrome-legged tables and lovingly reupholstered matching chairs parade brightly down the long room, while a crowd of smiling papier-mâché marionettes cha-cha around the ceiling, hundreds of them, grinning the cheerful fancies of the Mexican artisans who crafted them. "Going out for Mexican food is supposed to be fun and festive," says Rudy's owner, Barry Eastman. "I have fun collecting this stuff, and I like sharing it with my customers."

But while floor-to-ceiling whimsy may entice customers once, it's what comes out of the kitchen that lures them back. "The real fun in eating comes when you're served good food made from the best, freshest local ingredients," Barry maintains. He's convinced that food quality has been the key to his success for most of his fifteen years as an independent restaurateur. "The chains keep coming," he says, "but local buying gives me an edge. Their cooks are just warmer-uppers on an assembly line, handling pre-processed stuff from big institutional suppliers. Our cooks cook with pride; they make everything fresh, from scratch. And with that combination—good cooks and the best possible ingredients—you can educate your customers real fast."

Local producers supply 100 percent of the beef, chicken, pork, cheese, tortillas, tomatoes, garlic—even the flowers on the tables—at Rudy's,

generating $143,000 a year in sales. "Why eat a cardboard tomato from Florida, or beef that came from who-knows-where?" Barry asks. "Some experts will tell you it's about consistent supplies all year. Well, Iowa farmers are delivering all my major produce, even tomatoes, year around. The logistics are no big deal. Farmers want to bring their best, and they do; my local suppliers deliver right to the kitchen door."

The man making sure that the logistics of Rudy's produce supply are "no big deal" is University of Northern Iowa (UNI) faculty member Dr. Kamyar

Enshayan. An agricultural engineer by training, Kamyar discovered that his concern for environmental and social justice and economic opportunity blended with a desire to eat well. "I want to know what's in my food and that it's safe and wholesome for my family and me. I want to know who grew it, that they got a fair price, and that the water and soil are being protected," he declares, noting that "reconnecting people in a community with the land has become my profession now."

A grant from the Leopold Center for Sustainable Agriculture got Kamyar started on what is now UNI's Local Food Project. With three interested buyers—Rudy's, UNI's Dining Services, and Waterloo's Allen Hospital— Kamyar began scouting for suppliers at Black Hawk County farmers markets and meat lockers in spring 1997. "In our county there are fifty thousand households, spending roughly $370 million a year on food and beverages," he says. "For all Iowa families, it's nearly $5 billion a year, and most of that money leaves the state. But what if each family in our county spent an average of just $10 a week on locally grown foods? That would amount to more than $20 million dollars every year invested in local farms and businesses."

Although the UNI Local Food Project hasn't met Kamyar's "campaign goal" of a million dollars a month, the United States Department of Agriculture has recognized it as one of the dozen most successful efforts of its kind in the country. In addition to building an $800,000 sales network of twelve commercial buyers and twenty-seven suppliers, Kamyar and his students at UNI's Center for Energy and Environmental Education have promoted farmers markets, direct on-farm sales, and encouraged direct-to-home deliveries through CSAs (community supported agriculture associations).

Many people would buy more locally grown food if they knew where to get it, Kamyar's studies show, so the Local Foods Project is taking action. In 2003 they launched a Buy Fresh, Buy Local campaign in Black Hawk and neighboring counties to make it easier for residents in the region to find sources of locally grown food. They have also published and distributied 20,000 copies of a "get yourself a farmer" directory, which not only lists nearby sources of fruits, vegetables, poultry, eggs, and honey, but also includes local meat lockers, grocery stores, and restaurants selling local agricultural products. "My hope is that in a few years a frequently asked question among friends will be, 'So who is your farmer?'" Kamyar says. Reconnecting people with local sources of food, Kamyar declares, "is real homeland security." Barry Eastman sums it up this way: "The farmers who grow my produce are good friends of mine; they love to come in and see how we serve the stuff they grew. The guy who supplies my tomatoes and his family are regular customers. They'll come in, and their kids will say, 'That's ours! That's our food! We grew it!' and you can just about feel everybody in the place smiling."

WORKING TOGETHER FOR A BRIGHT FUTURE
Park View Inn & Suites and Conference Center

Mark Twain, the sage of Hannibal, Missouri, once declared, "Everybody talks about the weather, but nobody does anything about it."

Twain appreciated the beauty of rural America as much as anyone, and interpreted it with a keen sense of humor. He also had an insightful view of the world at large, born of the countryside with its fruited plains, fertile valleys, and clean, unbroken vistas that begin and end each day with the sun visible on the horizon.

To paraphrase Mr. Twain, at a time when just about everybody talks about their shrinking community and sagging economy, typically nobody does much about it—but not so in West Bend, Iowa. A couple of years ago, this small town in northwest Iowa reinvented itself in what has become something of a local tradition, and therein lies "the rest of the story."

West Bend is well known within the Midwest as the location of the Grotto of the Redemption, the inspiration of Father Paul Matthias Dobberstein. Father Dobberstein began building the grotto as a testament of faith in 1912 and kept building until his death in 1954. The structure has brought thousands of visitors to the town over the years, and the town flourished. But in recent years West Bend had struggled, as did many small Iowa towns. Agricultural markets were unfavorable, business activity was slack, school enrollment was declining, and tourism was down. In the fall of 1999, West Bend Economic Development invited area residents to a town meeting to address these pressing concerns.

This was not the first time the town had gathered to seek common solutions. Over the years, people in this small northwest Iowa community of 834 had come together numerous times to attract a professional or keep a business: a doctor's committee had brought a physician to town and a clinic was built. A search for an attorney had resulted in attracting one permanently, and so, too, an optometrist and a

dentist. When the dream was for a golf and country club, area residents organized to sell shares, acquire land, and build the West Bend Golf and Country Club. When the automobile dealership needed a new owner or it would have to close its doors, a group organized and sold shares to keep operating as West Bend Ford. Likewise, when the lumberyard was in the throes of closing down, a group stepped forward and sold shares in a new Community Lumber Supply. Now, somebody had to do something to forestall the slide of the local economy, and to begin to build a firm foundation for the future, if there was to be a future for the fair city.

After numerous meetings and countless jokes about "brainstorming, but without susceptible material," the proverbial light bulb went on for just about everybody involved. The group determined that the old 1950-vintage West Bend Motel could be replaced by a new motel and conference center, bringing tourists, business people, and community folks from miles around. With this idea in mind, the town residents formed a for-profit corporation, named a board of directors, and sold shares to finance the project. In just over a year, they received pledges for 412 shares at one thousand dollars each, and after a "name the new motel" contest, they named the motel Park View Inn & Suites. Vision Iowa funding met additional needs. With essential funding secured, ground was broken and construction began late in October 2001, with the hope that the motel would be open for business the following May 2002.

Construction proceeded amidst a wealth of cooperation among all involved including, to the surprise of all, the weather. It turned out to be a very un-Iowa winter, and every contractor worked diligently to meet the demanding schedule. Volunteers were enthusiastic and tireless in their devotion to the project. Friends and residents of the community donated money, furnishings and furniture, and decorations, and spent countless hours cleaning, painting, and installing right up to and beyond opening day. Their in-kind assistance far exceeded expectations.

One afternoon as construction proceeded, the now-deceased Reverend L. H. Greving, a builder and retired director of the Grotto, stopped by to take a look. Greving remembered how Father Dobberstein had said that the Grotto fulfilled a promise he had made in an hour of need, but that it also offered a promise of visitors, residents, and development for West Bend in a time of need. In Greving's words, "This is just a wonderful idea, because it is needed [by the community], and it is needed for our beautiful Grotto to be able to have more visitors."

The grand opening of the Park View Inn & Suites and Conference Center was held on schedule the first week of May 2002. Many visitors marveled at the uniqueness of design and the luxury of the accommodations, which were made possible thanks to the assistance of innumerable community volunteers. While everyone present seemed quite happy with the final product, one of the most telling and cherished comments came from a resident of a neighboring town: "Some of the other folks from my town who were here today wanted to know how little old West Bend could pull this off when we can't get our [substantially larger city] to work together to do much smaller joint projects."

The new Park View Inn & Suites and Conference Center has thirty-six rooms, including six appealing themed suites. Three suites contain whirlpool hot tubs, and two have fireplaces. All offer refrigerators and microwaves, and all but the attractive Honeymoon Suite have sleeper sofas. The Honeymoon Suite features romantic floral and cherub décor, king-sized bed, and hot tub. The Americana Suite of two rooms is decorated in patriotic style with king-sized bed and hot tub. The Safari Suite offers two rooms with a king bed, hot tub, and giraffe, hippo, monkey, and zebra wall paintings. The Fishing and Hunting Suites each have two queen beds, fireplaces, and suitable décor. The nautical Lighthouse Suite has extra space for a large family. All thirty-six rooms feature free high-speed Internet connections, and all outlets and telephone jacks are located for easy access.

The large 17-by-42-foot indoor swimming pool, whirlpool, sauna, and fitness rooms are a big hit with guests and community members as well. The party room is a multipurpose room for small meetings of up to forty persons, and the conference center is approved to seat 168 persons in comfort. The conference center can be divided into two smaller rooms, has high-speed Internet connectivity, a sound system for business clientele, and a podium.

Since opening, the Park View Inn & Suites, competently managed by Dawn Schmidt, has enjoyed a terrific response. Guests and visitors are very complimentary and congratulatory, and the town looks forward to more of the same as they continue to strive to make the new inn a place to stay and play— perchance to dream.

LOCALLY GROWN FOOD
DELIVERED TO YOUR DOOR
Sunflower Fields CSA

"I do this because it is the love of my life," Michael Nash says of his role in creating and operating Sunflower Fields CSA, a community supported agriculture operation in the northeast corner of Iowa. Sunflower Fields CSA is a collaborative organization of growers and producers who provide locally raised food to community residents.

Michael Nash and Solveig Hanson operate Sunflower Fields Farm near Waukon and coordinate the eleven-producer organization. Established in 1996, Sunflower Fields serves a rural community, a rarity among CSA operations, which normally operate in more urban areas. The organization's growers, producers, and shareholders (members who purchase "shares" of the farms' produce) note that Sunflower Fields CSA really stands for "community sustaining agriculture" because its goal is to serve and strengthen their community.

"Our purpose is to get top-quality, local food into the homes of people in our community at an affordable price," Michael says, "but the real rewards of this work are the positive contributions we make in our community and the relationships we have built with our shareholders. There is a mutual trust, and that is the single most important thing we do in our work to help sustain a rural community."

That philosophy of mutual trust is the primary reason for Sunflower Fields CSA's growth from 20 shareholders in 1996 to 225 in 2002. The operation has also grown from the initial Sunflower Fields vegetable farm to an eleven-producer organization that offers shareholders a range of fresh, locally produced foods including apples, berries, honey, eggs, chickens, and baked goods. Flower bouquets, herbs, tea, and homemade hand soap are also on the list of optional shares available.

"If you are a Sunflower Fields CSA shareholder, you absolutely know the people who are growing and producing your food because we deliver it to your door, and we discuss with you the thinking and the work and the challenges that went into it," Michael says. "You know where that food is grown, how it is grown, and how it is handled. You know that we are committed to providing you with good, healthful food that is locally produced with our own hands."

Sunflower Fields CSA delivers weekly boxes of vegetables and other items to the doors of about 195 of the 225 shareholders' homes. About thirty shareholders choose to stop by Sunflower Fields Farm or other CSA producer farms to pick up their weekly boxes. Delivered from mid-May into October, the boxes contain a variety of in-season, farm-fresh garden produce, plus any additional items shareholders have selected from the list of products offered by Sunflower growers and producers. Shareholders also receive a newsletter, recipes, and invitations to participate in special events.

Shareholder subscriptions range from $165 for the season for a single person share to $275 for large families. Affordability has always been a concern for the CSA, which is located in an economically struggling rural area. The CSA has been adaptable and creative in finding ways for families with limited incomes to be shareholders through work exchanges and other types of contributions in lieu of dollars.

The CSA holds special educational events and activities that have strengthened community bonds. Events at the farm include sessions on canning and preserving foods and "Rosie's Growers" (named after Sunflower Fields Farm's dog, Rosie), a program that teaches children from shareholder families about gardening, nutrition, cooking, and eating as a family. "That is the future of the local food system," Solveig says. "Programs like these educate children about the benefits and responsibilities of providing a community with nutritious, locally produced food."

The CSA also hosts a shareholder appreciation dinner in mid-October. "More than one hundred people were here for this fall's shareholders' dinner," says Solveig. That is an indication of the strength of the CSA community and its commitment to sustainable, local food production.

Diversity is the key to the successful operation of a farm that produces foods naturally, Michael says. His 215-acre farm grows about sixty-five different crops annually, not counting its hay production. About 42 acres are planted in trees, and other highly erodible slopes are used for pasture or have been enrolled in the Conservation Reserve Program and planted in switchgrass.

Cropland accounts for more than eighty acres of the farm's land, all contour-planted to minimize soil erosion. The cropland is divided into seven sectors, each of which cycles though a seven-year crop rotation. Each year two sectors are planted in vegetables, one in large grains, one in a cover crop, and three in hay.

"All agricultural practices break the natural cycles of the land," Michael says, "but our rule is, 'Don't break any cycles you don't have to break.'" To abide by this rule, Michael and Solveig are careful to match appropriate farming techniques with this hilly northeast Iowa region's native soils and tallgrass prairie history.

Visitors marvel at the beauty of the farm, which is located on a high hill offering spectacular views of the surrounding countryside. Shareholders are welcome to harvest surplus produce at no charge. The fact that many members choose to visit and "get their hands in the dirt" on the farm has as much to do with the beauty and the welcoming atmosphere of the place as the bonus vegetables.

Sunflower Fields CSA is moving forward with other programs to help put locally grown, healthful food on the tables of northeast Iowa people. Michael and Solveig are members of GROWN Locally (Goods Raised Only With Nature), which is a locally based farmer operated coop. GROWN Locally markets to institutional buyers such as nursing homes, schools, grocery stores, and restaurants. They are also upgrading facilities on the farm so that they will be able to cut, peel, and dice produce—and eventually can and freeze it—for commercial sale.

This collaboration of growers and producers who make up Sunflower Fields CSA in northeastern Iowa are committed to small, human-scale operations, their diverse character, and their place and purpose within the communities that surround them. They believe in the intrinsic need for good food, building relationships with the people in their region, the importance of quality products, and forming connections among all facets of their community.

RALLYING AROUND HABITAT RESTORATION
Ida County Communities Committed to Conservation

What began as an idea to improve pheasant hunting has become a countywide effort involving businesses, students, landowners, and hundreds of citizens in Ida County.

Since 1989, the local chapter of the nonprofit conservation organization Pheasants Forever has spent more than $500,000 to restore habitat on at least two-thirds of the county's seven hundred farms. In 2000, the group earned the state's Outstanding Chapter Award from the Iowa Department of Natural Resources (DNR).

The chapter's influence goes far beyond improvements in pheasant habitat. Students, church groups, and civic clubs that help with conservation tree plantings receive cash donations from the chapter.

When forty Ida Grove high school athletes, their coaches, the school principal, and the athletic director planted trees in a half-mile-long shelterbelt, radio station KIDA-FM broadcast live from the event.

"Pheasants Forever is also building a conservation ethic," explains Mike Mahn, Iowa DNR wildlife management biologist. When young people help with tree planting, they contribute to their community—parents welcome the enthusiasm in their youth, and support grows for the environment, he asserts.

Schools in Ida County have developed outdoor classrooms with help from the local Pheasants Forever chapter. The chapter has given books to libraries,

supported the Battle Hill Museum of Natural History in Battle Creek, and contributed to scholarship funds at three high schools in the county. The chapter helped Ida Grove develop the multipurpose Pleasant Valley Trail and seeded native grasses near the city's hospital. One way or another, Pheasants Forever touches most residents of the county.

Each March, businesses donate money, merchandise, and employee time for the annual fund-raising banquet. "For our little county, we try to put on kind of a big show," remarks chapter treasurer Rusty Sadler. Even with a county population of fewer than eight thousand, the Pheasants Forever banquet draws about eight hundred people. The prime rib dinner is served at the Skate Palace in Ida Grove, which is the only facility big enough to handle the crowd.

The gala includes families, with games and activities for the kids. Along with auction items and prizes such as golf vacations, all-terrain vehicles, dog food, and wildlife prints that appeal more to the men, there are special prizes and jewelry for the women. Hunters who come to Ida County in the fall from as far away as Georgia sometimes return for the spring banquet to show their appre-ciation for Iowa hospitality. The event grosses about $140,000.

"The banquet requires months of planning," says chapter president Rich Smith, who delegates jobs to fifteen or twenty board members. Volunteers plan the meal, print programs, recruit kitchen help, and solicit donations. Rich explains that it is relatively easy to obtain contributions from businesses because they see how wildlife, hunting, and tourism benefit the people, communities, and economy of the county.

Success breeds success. "You show them what you've done," says Rich. "Donors like the idea of local people reinvesting locally raised money in local projects."

Landowners are Pheasants Forever's biggest supporters, says Lorne Miller, district conservationist for the Natural Resources Conservation Service (NRCS). "We've just about got people knocking down the doors wanting to be a part of planting trees or doing something good for habitat on their farms," he says. Ida County farmers take pride in the wildlife on their land. Lorne's goal is a habitat project on every farm in the county.

Even some farmers who once were lukewarm to wildlife and hunters now welcome the conservation efforts, explains farmer and Pheasants Forever board member Mason Fleenor. "It isn't just the hunting; it's the people," he says.

Projects jointly sponsored by Pheasants Forever, the NRCS, the Ida County Conservation Board, and the Iowa DNR, among other groups, make up an impressive list: 150,000 trees planted, 300 miles of terraces seeded, 4,700 acres of native grasses established, 172 food plots created, 161 acres of riparian buffer strips formed.

But the group counts its success in results, rather than numbers, notes Rhett Leonard, director of the Ida County Conservation Board. "They really seem to put the time and effort and money into doing it right," he explains. Instead of just giving landowners trees, for example, the chapter will loan a farmer a power auger to dig holes, and pay a service group to help with planting.

"All their tree plantings have weed mats and their hardwoods have tree shelters to try to ensure the livability," Rhett explains. "They've gone that extra step and done the follow-up. Then you've actually got something after five years!"

Rhett also praises the emphasis on youth and education. Each year, the chapter gives a tree to every fifth grader in the county. They have sponsored birdhouse workshops, paid for student field trips, given supplies to naturalists, and donated money for a county conservation board education complex.

Members also go pheasant hunting with local youth. The youngsters, who first must complete a hunter safety course, receive an orange vest and cap, shooting instruction, the chance to hunt with a bird dog, and help with cleaning and packaging game.

"It's the type of thing so, so many of us take for granted," Rich says. But many Pheasants Forever members want "to give something back."

Rich's leadership has sparked the chapter, says Rusty Sadler. "He really has a clear vision and knows how to keep things moving." Rusty also praises GOMACO, the concrete construction equipment manufacturer where Rich works as vice president of administration and finance. The company supports Pheasants Forever with financial contributions and the time spent by Rich and other employees.

Many other businesses, such as Hultgren Implement, the John Deere dealership where Rusty works, and Midwest Industries, which builds boat hoists and trailers, also contribute money and employee time to Pheasants Forever.

The strength of Pheasants Forever also helps build political support for conservation, reports Don Poggensee, who is a member of the Ida County Conservation Board. "You get six hundred or seven hundred people together and politicians start paying attention," he says.

The secret, Rich says, is people. With good landowner relationships, visible projects, outreach to other groups, energetic members, and cooperation with government agencies, even a small group of dedicated people can have a big impact.

TOMATILLOS AMONG THE SOYBEANS
Diversity Gardens in Lenox

"Put a stick on the end of it, put mayonnaise on it, parmesan cheese, and hot sauce, and it is so good!" Veronica Cruz stands amid corn, tomatillo, cilantro, and a wealth of chili pepper plants and explains a uniquely Latino twist to preparing Iowa's summertime favorite, corn-on-the-cob.

One section of the garden is fenced off from the rest and seems to say, "For Kids Only." This is where the children come every Monday night for a gardening lesson. The scarecrow the children made stands watch over the plot, his blue jean pants and plaid shirt rippling in the breeze. Tin plates rattle and clatter against the metal fencing.

Here in this small southwestern Iowa town of Lenox stands a community garden like many others that are springing up around the state in both rural and urban areas. "We had several main objectives for this garden," says Tim Ennis, executive director of Ag Connect, the nonprofit organization that helped start the gardens here. "We saw it as a benefit to the participants for their personal consumption and satisfaction. And we wanted to connect nonfarmers to agriculture and acquaint them with some of the

larger commercial opportunities of local agriculture, such as selling at farmers markets."

But it was a third objective that named the garden. As Ag Connect project manager Bill Beaman explains, while this is primarily an effort to add diversity to Iowa's crop base, it is also fostering diversity in the cultural landscape. Hence, the project has been dubbed "Diversity Gardens." While plots are available to all community members, most of the gardeners here are new immigrants interested in growing foods particular to their home cuisine. In Lenox, the proportion of Latino residents has risen in ten years to 25 percent of the town's total 1,360 residents. Most come from Mexico and Texas to work in one of the nation's largest egg-processing plants, owned by Michael Foods.

"We wanted to encourage produce other than conventional corn and soybeans," Beaman says. "The neat thing about this is that these new people in town are willing to look at new ideas."

Lenox residents try to be inclusive of their new neighbors, Bill says. "At the church I go to, we've made efforts to incorporate Hispanics into our masses. But it takes years for people to learn to grow together. The garden seemed like something we could do and grow together and enjoy doing," he says.

The Lenox Development Corporation donated the land and had a water hydrant put in. Plants were donated by businesses and organizations—a nearby nursery, the FFA in Corning, a high school agricultural education class, even the horticulture students and their instructor at Western Iowa Tech Community College in Sioux City. Someone brought a roto tiller to prepare the planting site. Local master gardeners offered their expertise and organized educational activities for the children's garden. "Lenox is kind of proud of it," Bill says. "The volunteers are great. You never have to ask twice."

As a member of the Latino community, Veronica was quick to see the benefits the garden could hold for families like hers. "Having the garden is one of the most wonderful things that could happen here," Veronica remarks. "The garden makes the Latinos feel welcome in this community." Feeling a part of the community, they are more likely to put down roots, buy a home, and raise their families, a concept their employers at Michael Foods actively promotes, she says.

Veronica's bilingual and organizing skills were invaluable for involving

Latinos. She herself came from Texas with her husband and six children five years ago, seeking jobs at the egg-processing plant. She got involved in the gardens because she thought it would be good for the Latino community. And she urged her Latino friends to participate, giving them rides to the garden to plant, weed, or harvest, and sharing in the joy of having fresh produce for cooking.

"I got a group of ladies together and explained all we have to do is take care of this garden. They're going to provide everything," Veronica says. "The ladies made a list of what they wanted. They really liked the idea of it."

"The best part is the way it brings people together," Veronica observes. "It's hard for people to make time to go out to the gardens because everyone is so busy, but I call them and offer them a ride. And then once we are out there, we have so much fun! Some of the ladies went out and got chilies from the garden, and they got so much attention for making their enchiladas with them."

The Lenox gardeners have successfully marketed fresh produce at the local farmers market and are talking of making and selling salsa. "I think there is a growing demand for local foods," Tim says. "The gardens help meet a need in the market for locally grown foods and entertainment produce, such as pumpkins and decorative corn. It makes the future supply for farmers markets have a broader base."

That Glorious Song of Old

Essay by Mary Swander

SQUEEZED together on the hard wooden benches in the meeting room of the country schoolhouse, we sang Christmas carols, a slow, modal sound echoing off the plain pine walls. *It came upon a midnight clear.* Outside, the storm cocooned us in snow, the flakes swirling through the darkness, covering the horses at the hitching post. It was the night of the Christmas program in my neighborhood, a rural Iowa community where I am one of the few "English," or non-Amish. Several families were delayed, their sleighs inching over waist-high drifts. Mahlon, the minister, kept us singing, his hand moving up and down with a steady rhythm. *That glorious song of old.*

Then some older boys extinguished the kerosene lanterns hanging from ceiling hooks. Our voices hushed. A chorus of young voices arose from the basement steps, the notes pure and clear. Thirteen Amish children and their teacher—who couldn't have been more than eighteen years old—wound through the meeting room. Each child carried a single white candle, the light glowing in the darkness. *With angels bending toward the earth.*

The candles were snuffed, the lanterns re-lit and the children went into a sing-song rhyming recitation of a poem dedicated to "Grandma." Just one grandma? I thought. There have to be others here. The room was packed with older women, their shawls draped over their shoulders, their white hair pulled back into buns. But when the poem was finished, just one grandma stood up and bowed. She was the ancestor of all the children, these siblings and cousins smiling out at us with the same grin that swept across the old woman's face.

Outside the window of this one-room schoolhouse, the wind swept across the pastures and cornfields where this same ancestry, this same sense of community, keeps the face of the land intact. Here, near Kalona, Iowa, the largest Amish settlement west of the Mississippi, the farms are small, averaging around 120 acres, the houses nestled into the rolling hills, one close enough to another to hear the voices of children carried through the clear air from one farmstead to the next. The farmhouses are large, white, boxy structures with wrap-around porches and room for at least ten people at the dining room table. Most farmsteads have "Grandpa" houses, smaller structures that quarter elderly relatives, a loom or quilting frame often set up in the main room. The well-kept barns are painted bright red, their lofts filled with hay, their stalls with Holsteins. Every Monday morning, clothes flap in the breeze: a chorus line of denim pant legs dancing in the wind.

When the snow melts, the gardens are tilled, their rich, composted soils planted with peas, lettuce, and spinach. Earthworms wiggle through the dirt dotted with plastic milk jugs, or mini-hothouses, encasing cabbage and broccoli seedlings. The manured fields are plowed under, teams of draft horses or old tractors preparing the land for a four-crop rotation of corn, beans, oats, and alfalfa. Hay is still baled as it was in the 1950s, in squares with binders. The wagons wobbling down the road on their metal rims are piled high with their bounty. Oats are stacked to dry in shocks before threshing, and in midsummer, the play of light across the bundles creates a mirage of earth tones that rivals a Monet painting. During fall harvest, you can still find whole families picking corn by hand or slaughtering their own hogs and canning the meat, the pressure cooker steaming on the stove.

During any season, one can immediately grasp the health and prosperity of the region. Bankruptcies from debts for purchases of large machinery and additional tracts of land are virtually nonexistent. No beer cans litter the ditches. No old cars or washing machines trash the creeks. Instead, the grid of gravel roads carries buggy, buckboard, and sleigh travel, the horses trotting along through dust, mud, and snow. The grid of human relationships carries a five-hundred-year-old agricultural way of life, its successes trotting through depressions and farm crises. The farms, like the families in this region, are tightly knit together by a set of spiritual beliefs that embraces the sustainability of the land and the importance of community.

At the turn of the millennium, the Amish are a blast from the past for most of us who have no concept of one-room schools and a gathering of people with a common ancestor. Yet many baby boomers are on a quest to find a better way of life in our society. Our postmodern culture has given us more career options, more education, and more mobility and independence than our grandparents enjoyed, but it has also left us with a malaise. We are weary of moving from one job to the next, from one city to the next, where the only constant is the familiar McDonald's sign. We are frantic with the responsibilities that have funneled down to us, trying to single-handedly care for our own growing children while at the same time caring for our aging parents. We distrust institutions and dread turning over the end of our own lives to nursing homes and assisted living centers. We long for a stronger sense of community and connection, a desire to at least know our neighbors' names.

So co-housing and intentional communities are springing up all over the United States. Clusters of people are founding communities addressing a variety of special needs: gays, the disabled, artists, and organic farmers. Whether in rural or urban settings, people are attempting to reckon with their isolation and loneliness, trying to cope with their lack of extended families. The boomers want to create a sense of community with more organization, structure, and continuity than the communes of their youth.

Most of these intentional communities are filled with entrepreneurs who desire to interact with their neighbors in a cooperative way. When you click on the websites of a sampling of these successful communities, whether a chic enclave in Santa Fe or a clutch of trailers parked in the Monzano Mountains in New Mexico, you discover threads of the Amish philosophy. These communities are stitched together by common values or spiritual beliefs. They often pool resources and undertake cooperative tasks. Many of these communities are urban and simply desire a saner way to live together in clusters of families. Others are rural communities involved in raising organic livestock, in truck farming, and in CSAs.

If agriculture were indeed rethinking its sense of scope, it would also do well to rethink its sense of community. If new farmers hope to carry the light of single candles into the darkness, they must also renew their relationships with their neighbors. The Amish way of life can provide an example of an agrarian tradition that through the cohesiveness of its people has done much to preserve the land. The "quaint" Amish, with their nostalgic window into the past, have become a model for the future.

Mary Swander is a writer and distinguished professor at Iowa State University's Department of English. Her latest book is The Desert Pilgrim: En Route to Mysticism and Miracles, *from Viking, 2003.*

CHAPTER EIGHT
Learning

If there is a single theme that unifies the chapters of this book, it is the central role of learning in the lives of the people whose stories are told in its pages. The farmers, marketers, product innovators, alternative energy producers, and conservationists described have all had to learn new ways of doing things and new ways of communicating with their fellow community members. Whether their learning means acquiring specific skills or more generally working toward newly established community goals, virtually every one is a learner of one kind or another.

The learning of these community members is not likely to end soon, not as long as their commitment remains firm. Advances in technical expertise will be important in the development of new products and new techniques. And beyond specific skill sets, a kind of community learning will be essential as well. In this chapter, we hear the voices of men and women pursuing lifelong learning in a very practical sense—creating meaningful lives in harmony with the environment that sustains them.

SLOW FOOD IN IOWA CITY
Chef Kurt Friese and Devotay

Kurt Friese remembers when, as a kid growing up in Columbus, Ohio, his dad took him to the grand opening of Wendy's very first restaurant. Today, fast food has become so antithetical to his values, that he may never again eat another corporately cooked burger.

Kurt and his wife, Kim McWane Friese, have become Iowa's gurus for a concept that has spread from Europe to the United States and that is taking solid root in the Midwest: Slow Food. Kurt is extraordinarily convincing because every day the fruits of his labor are testimony to his philosophy.

Kurt is the chef and owner of a restaurant in Iowa City: Devotay. There are certain menu items you will never see at the Frieses' establishment. The ubiquitous commercial potato chip and perfectly shaped pickles do not adorn the plate. Coke, Pepsi, and 7-Up are not offered. Forget about the omnipresent cellophane-wrapped peppermint. In his restaurant, Kurt uses only ingredients that are locally produced, or produced by noncorporate farmers and suppliers. Wild mushrooms, freshly baked sourdough bread, fresh mozzarella, and field greens from Iowa City's farmers market or Kim's garden are standbys. The fresh chevre cheese comes from a local goat farmer, the chocolate caramel pecan cheesecake is made by his friend Colleen, and the pork comes from the nearby Niman Ranch–affiliated producer.

"The way to make the best possible food," Kurt says, "is to start with local and fresh ingredients. It's not so much politics as pocketbook. You get a lot more accolades—and more customers coming back—because your food tastes fresher."

But Kurt's passion is clearly as much about his politics as it is his pocketbook. The founder of Iowa's first Slow Food chapter—or convivium (Latin for feast or banquet)—Kurt has become an effective educator about the Slow Food philosophy.

The Slow Food movement began in Italy in 1986 when writer Carlo Petrini rebelled against a new McDonald's opening at the Piazza Di Spagna in Rome. The movement has grown to more than eighty thousand members in seven hundred chapters in sixty countries. Slow Food is more about a deliberate, conscious understanding of where food comes from and who is benefiting from its purchase than it is about the time it takes to prepare it. "Slow food doesn't mean using your crock pot," Kurt is quick to point out. "You can prepare 'slow' food in just a few minutes."

Food is more than fuel, Kurt explains. It is our heritage, our tradition, and the way we express love to our families. "Somehow, the industrialized world convinced itself that cooking is a chore, on a level with laundry and window washing," he says. "We have lost so much in this country in the last fifty or sixty years as a result of the industrialized standardization of taste. We've sacrificed huge amounts of our culture for the sake of what is called 'convenience.' We've mistaken frenzy for efficiency."

"Generations of children are growing up not knowing how to cook, never eating fresh, locally produced food, and never understanding where food comes from," maintains Kurt. Fast-food marketing has been enormously successful and Kurt is sharply critical of its messages. "Food franchises tell us that they are our neighborhood bar and grill," he says. "But they are not. It's a lie."

Passionately literal about what it means to buy from one's neighbors, Kurt insists on buying almost all of his services from local business people. "I buy my insurance, get my car serviced, and bank from my neighbors—not from giant corporations," he says. "Rural communities are viable when people trade with each other and keep dollars in the local economy. The same people I buy from eat at my restaurants and help me send my kids to college. Trading with and serving one's neighbors results in a commitment to quality." Kurt continues, "There is something almost spiritual about knowing where our food comes from and being able to shake the hands of the farmers who produced it."

The moment you step into Devotay, a small rustic restaurant in the University of Iowa's campus town, you know this is no franchise. Tables, chairs, and china are a wild and mismatched assortment, and the restaurant is decorated with Kim McWane Friese's work (in addition to being a Slow Food guru, Kim is also an accomplished potter). The menu is sophisticated, and Kurt—always the educator—provides a glossary. (Mahon is a Spanish cheese similar to Parmesan but softer. Oloroso Seco is a type of dark, semisweet sherry. Alioli is garlic mayonnaise.) The variety and complexity of foods rival those found at the finest East Coast restaurants. Kurt's second restaurant, Adagio (Italian for "slow"), opened in October 2001 and featured foods of the northern Mediterranean. It was twice as big as the cozy Devotay and offered a more elegant décor. Unfortunately, it could not compete against the multitude of large, wealthy chains on the west side and closed in May 2003.

Although slowing down in all areas of life is his ideal, Kurt admits that owning a restaurant makes it difficult to live slowly. But he loves to cook and says he could find no profession more rewarding than giving instant pleasure to a gratified consumer. He and Kim have two children. When his teenage son wants to step over the time-honored adolescent/parental line-in-the-sand, he eats at a fast-food restaurant. "I pretend to be angry," Kurt says with a smile.

The Slow Food movement gives Kurt an avenue to teach new understanding about eating and to provide alternative eating experiences. He is a frequent guest on public radio, edits an e-magazine called *Mangiare*, and authors columns in three local newspapers. In the fall of 2002, Iowa City's Slow Food convivium launched a four-day Field to Family festival that featured entertainment by nationally known authors, a culinary walk, farm tours, cooking demonstrations, and a gala dinner made of local ingredients.

Kurt has found Iowans warmly receptive to Slow Food, which, after all, is what farmers have been practicing for years. Iowa recently started its second Slow Food convivium in Des Moines. "I didn't expect to have so much success spreading the word," remarks Kurt. "When I'm a guest on radio talk shows, I keep expecting to hear from fast-food fans or owners, but it has never happened."

HOOKING PEOPLE ON LAND USE ISSUES

LaVon Griffieon and 1000 Friends of Iowa

Soybeans have popped up among newly planted perennials near Community Baptist Church, rebuilt after arsonists destroyed the gathering place in one of Des Moines' poorest neighborhoods.

Community activist LaVon Griffieon smiles and explains that a few soybeans must have been in the bottom of her husband's grain truck when they used it to haul fifteen loads of compost to the site of a landscape renovation project. It may have been an accidental planting, but it's also a sign of the growing link between suburban sprawl and urban renewal.

"What I've come to realize is that rural Iowa and urban areas have a lot in common," says LaVon, president and cofounder of 1000 Friends of Iowa, a grassroots organization formed in 1998 to educate Iowans about urban sprawl and promote responsible land use. "We are all important to each other."

LaVon's struggle began more than a dozen years earlier on the rural end of the spectrum—the Century Farm that she and her husband, Craig, tend on the edge of Ankeny. Their four children are the fifth generation to live in the white, two-story farmhouse, and the sixth generation to be on the land. They farm about twelve hundred acres, raising corn, soybeans, oats and hay, a cow-calf herd of thirty-five to forty head, and a feeder beef operation. They also raise pastured poultry (chickens and turkeys), which they direct market to local customers.

But in their neighborhood, rich farmland is quickly giving way to development. Residential subdivisions have sprung up and a convenience store has opened nearby. Two golf courses are within a mile of the farm and a third is being built. The Ankeny city limits touch the Griffieon property.

LaVon's first attempt to save her farm heritage was to share it with others via a classroom education program. "I thought that if I could educate the kids I could get ahead of the urban sprawl," she explains.

Her Ag in the Classroom program began in 1988 with a class of fourth-grade students in Ankeny. She wrote letters every month about what was happening on the farm, and the students would write back. Soon she was corresponding with twenty-one classrooms throughout Polk County, making videos, and hosting busloads of schoolchildren. In thirteen years, she led more than twelve thousand children and adults on tours of her farm.

"I still was pretty distraught with all the development pressure," she continues. "People would tell me, 'Well, LaVon, that's progress and you can't stop progress.' My question was, 'Progress toward what?'"

"We have something very special here in Iowa, our climate and our soils," she says. "We are lucky to live in an environment so conducive to food production in a world where, for many millions of people, such conditions only exist in prayers."

Her frustration continued to mount. In 1996—she can name the date, July 18, and picture the people in her living room—she organized a meeting. The guests included conservationists, people involved in her church's urban housing program, and representatives from the offices of Senators Harkin and Grassley, the Leopold Center for Sustainable Agriculture, and Iowa State University.

"We sat in a circle and simply went around the room, sharing our thoughts about what was happening," she explains. "At the end, we all decided that

what we really needed was a way to educate people, to get the word out, so we formed a speakers bureau. Out of that meeting we later developed 1000 Friends of Iowa."

The idea for the grassroots organization was to have one thousand members, each contributing one hundred dollars toward an annual one hundred thousand dollar budget to educate Iowans about land use. After four years, the group already has 960 members and small grants to tackle

various projects throughout the state. Which brings LaVon to the urban end of the spectrum.

In 2000, 1000 Friends had outgrown the Griffieon's two-story farmhouse and the 1890 Victorian inner-city home of cofounder Ed Fallon. They had just received a W.K. Kellogg Foundation grant for a revitalization project in Des Moines' River Bend neighborhood, and they needed a base from which to guide volunteer activities. They found the right fit in nearby Highland Park, a culturally diverse community north of the river. The building they rent for an office had once been a drugstore, then a head shop, which closed due to illegal drug-related activity.

LaVon likes to talk about the area's history and how the neighborhood has survived through the years.

"This used to be a city with its own school district and municipal water plant, even a college, until it was annexed by the City of Des Moines with seven other communities in 1899," she says. "The railroad brought people to the area and sparked four decades of development beginning in 1870."

The community was unable to fight annexation, then was hit by development of area shopping malls, all drawing business away from Highland Park. But the community spirit seems unsinkable. A directory of businesses in the Highland Park, Oak Park, and Union Park neighborhoods shows page after page of locally owned ventures. The directory, developed by 1000 Friends, is being delivered door-to-door to 6,500 households in the area.

The $150,000 Kellogg Foundation grant to 1000 Friends for the River Bend project was a major boost. It includes money to landscape eight lots in the 1300 block of Seventh Street where 1000 Friends had hoped to spark interest in a community grocery store to sell Iowa-grown foods. Although the community store plan was rejected in favor of a supermarket, five homes were moved from the construction site to other vacant lots. The block, which has a homeless shelter and a church mission, now has homes for nine new families and thirty-five partners working on community garden plots, an arbor, and a playground.

LaVon enthusiastically shares plans for native prairie plantings designed to improve the soil, rain gardens to collect and retain runoff, and trees for both residential as well as commercial lots. "We've been treating our urban soils like

dirt," she says. "The topsoil is stripped off, the clay is compacted until it is like cement. Conservation efforts have been successful on agricultural land for the past fifty years and I think it is time to bring that knowledge to town. We need to protect our soils and water, no matter where they are located."

LaVon says the farm tours and urban gardens have one thing in common. "These are things that hook people on land use issues," she says, adding that her goal is to help people understand the need for land use legislation— for wealthy suburbs as well as culturally diverse inner city neighborhoods.

"You can't wait until this is biting you in the butt," she says. "You have to look at the big picture."

EMPOWERING ENTREPRENEURS
Penny Brown Huber and Growing Your Small Market Farm

Self confidence. According to Penny Brown Huber, that's the most important lesson of her Drake University entrepreneurship course for small-market farmers. "I try to empower them. At first, when they say 'I'm a farmer,' there's an implication that they are not quite in business," she says. "We want them to understand they are business people first."

Students in Penny's class quickly discover that along with learning traditional accounting methods and how to write a business plan, they have to learn to be bold. Sometimes Penny will work with them at a farmers market booth to help them think about their selling techniques. "I tell them, if someone comes up and says, 'Your tomatoes are a dollar a pound too much,' and you know that you have priced them fairly, then you need to politely articulate the value of your product—to be able to say in effect, 'This is valuable produce that I have raised myself,'" Penny explains.

Penny recalls working with fruit-and-vegetable farmer Angela Tedesco. "We were going to sell her strawberries and raspberries at our farmers market

booth. I priced her strawberries at $4.00 a quart, and her raspberries at $4.00 a pint. Angela said 'Maybe you should put them at $3.50 and $3.00.' But we knew they were a very difficult organic crop to raise, and she had an outstanding food product," Penny remarks.

"We had customers coming to the booth saying, 'Four dollars for a pint of raspberries, are you kidding?' We would explain the food value of the berries but if they still didn't want to buy, we had to be willing to let them leave the booth without buying. The quality of the produce was high, so every Saturday within two hours of the opening of the market we had all her strawberries and raspberries sold. Once folks tried them, some would buy four or six pints of raspberries at a time."

So part of the class is building the students' personal strength, building them up about the important work they're doing. "You know, we always think of farmers as nice and kind, but when you're a business person, it's about money, and I tell them, 'I know it sounds harsh, but at the end of the day, you have to feed your family, pay your bills, and feel good about what you're doing,'" Penny explains.

Penny's understanding of the need for farmers to have a clear sense of their own value was born of her personal entrance into the business of farming. Equipped with a master's degree in public administration and several years of working to develop her own small business, she started thinking she would like to try her hand as a farmer. Knowledgeable about the assistance available for entrepreneurs in the commercial business world, she searched for similar resources for would-be farmers, but ended feeling frustrated. "It was obscure," she recalls. "In the business sector, the training is more succinct, and I thought, 'Why don't we have this in agriculture?'"

Penny approached Neil Hamilton, director of the Drake Agricultural Law Center, who gave her the go ahead to develop a program—providing she could raise the funding for a three-year program, a task that would have closed the door in the minds of less determined folks. Within a year, Penny had secured the necessary funding from the USDA-Rural Development, Iowa Department of Economic Development, Iowa Agricultural Development Authority, Iowa Farm Bureau Federation, Iowa State University Extension, and Iowa Department of Agriculture and Land Stewardship.

Growing Your Small Market Farm, the resulting program, is now a one-year course. From February through April, the students meet to work through the curriculum, write business plans, and learn accounting methods using QuickBooks Pro. For the following six months—the busiest season for farmers—students receive one-on-one assistance. During this time Penny makes at least one site visit to each student's farm and helps them solve one clearly defined problem. The course wraps up with group meetings and reports in November.

For the most part, class members are non-traditional college students. Many have established businesses, but at least one was in high school. Jason Heki started raising chickens as a hobby when he was fourteen. After seeing a newspaper ad for the class, he decided to turn his hobby into a business. "It's really a good class for anyone starting a business. It helped me see all the start-up costs and how to market my product," Jason says.

Jason discovered that there was a good market and premium prices paid for chemical-free vegetables and eggs from free-range chickens. "For as little as I can do compared with a very large producer, I can get a better price," Jason explains. After two years in business, Jason is expanding to include antibiotic free, free-range broiler chickens and hopes to keep running the business while attending college.

The business plan Jason wrote in the class not only guided his fledgling business but gained him national recognition. The plan earned first place in a statewide competition sponsored by the John Papajohn Entrepreneurial Center, and Jason received honorable mention as Entrepreneur of the Year from the National Coalition for Empowering Youth Entrepreneurs (NCEYE).

A well-developed business plan also brought results for class members Nan Bonfils and Don Adams, who run Full Circle Farm near Madrid. After developing their business plan, the volume of their farm sales doubled and their customer base tripled. At the same time, they learned to think wisely about evaluating their profitability. "Increased sales don't necessarily translate into increased profitability. It's tempting to kid yourself about the true cost of production. A thorough business plan won't let this happen," Nan explains.

It was this kind of careful analysis that made the class valuable to Maury Wills, who farms with his wife, Mary, on thirty-two acres west of Adel. Along with tending his organic apple orchard, Maury works full time for the Iowa Department for Agriculture and Land Stewardship. "It's easy when you have a day job to subsidize a small business like this instead of treating it as a money-maker. This class made me very conscious of the financial aspects because I want it to be a profit-making business," he says. Initially Maury took the class because he wanted to produce organic applesauce. But after taking the class, he decided to go more slowly and improve his production methods before expanding into a new area.

Watching the progress of the students in her class gives Penny a feeling of accomplishment. "Everyone in the class last year, it's like they're on a rocket ship," she observes. "It is so amazing. They begin with a lot of things swirling in their heads about what they want to do and this class gets them focused. I just think of it as helping people."

CULTIVATING A SPIRITUAL CONNECTION TO THE EARTH

Prairiewoods Franciscan Spirituality Center

Go, eat your bread with enjoyment and drink your wine with a merry heart; for God has approved of what you do.   Ecclesiastes: 9–7

Prairiewoods Franciscan Spirituality Center is built on a stone-solid belief: people have an ethical imperative to cherish the Earth. Located in Hiawatha, Iowa, on the north edge of Cedar Rapids, the primary message of the center is that our culture and civilization will survive the twenty-first century only if we honor our spiritual connection with the Earth. People and their works must be integral with the natural world and must exist in communion with the Earth.

"Our goal is to bring spirituality and ecology together," says Sister Betty Daugherty, a leader of the ten-member professional staff of Prairiewoods. She notes that the work of Prairiewoods is influenced by the philosophy of Thomas Berry, theologian and historian who has studied and written on human cultures and their relations with the natural world.

The seventy-acre tract of Prairiewoods has been maintained by the Franciscan Sisters since the 1960s and has been the site of the spirituality center since it was founded in 1995. Prairiewoods is described as "a sacred place in which all faiths can join together to explore relationships with God, the Earth, themselves, and others." It is a center for spirituality, ecology, and holistic living.

The center's professional staff help raise awareness of people's responsibility for and commitment to an environmental ethic based on reverence for the Earth, the moral values of conservation, a sense of community, and the life of obligation, commitment, and sacrifice.

Prairiewoods offers counseling, retreat facilities, resources, and programs that advocate for the environment and ecological justice. The staff offer courses in theology, spirituality, psychology, and ecology—all with a core link to an environmental ethic. Prairiewoods hosts numerous retreats, including the 2001 and 2002 Energy Expo conducted by the Iowa Renewable Energy Association (I-RENEW).

Prairiewoods environmental outreach programs help manifest ethical ideals, values, and words into actions. Staff have made presentations and conducted workshops on environmentally sound lawn care—especially for children's day care centers. Of the twenty-five day care center operators who attended a 2002 workshop, twenty-four altered their lawn care practices to reduce children's exposure to herbicides and other chemicals.

Prairiewoods "Food and Faith" presentations at area churches encourage people to support local farmers. The presentations have resulted in dozens of people joining CSA (community supported agriculture) organizations, shopping at local farmers markets, and seeking out locally produced and processed meats.

For three years, one of Prairiewoods's environmental outreach programs has been a project to encourage Iowa church congregations to use Iowa-produced wines for their communion rites. Jonna Higgins-Freese, former coordinator of environmental outreach, conceived the idea when she read the "Grape Expectations" report on the Iowa grape industry, commissioned by the Leopold Center for Sustainable Agriculture.

LEARNING

"It just seemed to be a natural connection," Jonna says. "Churches are among the most receptive places to talk about the spiritual and ethical values of environmental programs—and many churches purchase Eucharist wine. Usually that purchase is made by the church's altar guild, and selection is based on what is cheapest. But if this wine is the substance that is or represents the blood of Christ, shouldn't it be something that promotes justice and peace and sense of community?" Jonna remarks.

Jonna took the church Eucharist wine proposal to the Leopold Center and was invited by the Southeast Iowa Synod of the Evangelical Lutheran Church in America to help organize a vineyard field day for pastors and ministers of Iowa congregations. Held at the Tabor Home Winery and Vineyard near Baldwin, Iowa, the field day was a successful introduction of the benefits and ethical justice of buying locally produced wine for communion. About fifteen pastors participated and heard the appeal for supporting local producers.

Iowa currently has twenty bonded wineries: six estate wineries that grow wine-making grapes in their own vineyards and fourteen other wineries that produce wines from fruits. "The state's grape industry is growing," Jonna remarks, "but its continued success depends on local consumers purchasing Iowa wines rather than wines made in other states." Winemaking is truly a "value-added" enterprise for vineyard owners. So churches—and more important, members of church congregations who are made aware of the Iowa wine issue—can be a positive force in the success of the local grape industry.

There are also strong environmental and eco-justice motivations for buying Iowa wines. The largest percentage of wine purchased in Iowa is produced in

California, where large vineyards are regularly sprayed with pesticides and where the fieldwork is done predominantly by migrant workers who receive low wages. "When people buy Iowa wines," Jonna notes, "they support a grape industry that is more caring of the Earth and people."

Another benefit of buying Iowa wines is that you get to experience the regional flavor of different varieties. "That's the beauty of wine," says Jonna, "it's so local and so dependent on its environment." Discovering a new favorite from a local winery is a pleasure that far surpasses the monotony in the taste of mass-produced wines.

"The local communion wine project has been a limited success which needs advocates to keep it going," Jonna explains. "Leadership of altar guilds changes every year, and when the new person asks, 'Why are we spending eleven dollars for local wine when we can buy Mogan David for six dollars?' the eco-justice and environmental reasons need to be introduced again." While the exact number of congregations using Iowa wines for communion has not been tracked, Jonna estimates that more than two dozen currently do. "But probably the biggest benefit of the communion wine project is that it was a hook," Jonna explains. "It got people thinking about the importance of buying locally produced foods."

Since the work of Prairiewoods is translating spiritual purpose into hands-on action, it is fitting that communion wine, the symbolic blood of the bond of body, spirit, and faith, has become a symbol of the center's work for environmental and social justice in Iowa's rural communities.

SOME THINGS YOU CAN'T LEARN IN A CLASSROOM

Iowa State University's Life in Iowa Program

Spring term 2003 ends at Iowa State University, and sixty-four undergraduate students head out to prepare for their future by living, working, and studying in towns and rural areas across Iowa. This is place-based education, learning that is rooted in the unique local culture and environment of a particular place, and it represents a bold new educational initiative called Life in Iowa.

The lush, rolling hills of Adair County have welcomed two Life in Iowa students. In the county seat of Greenfield, interior design major Jennifer Norman works with the local Main Street Iowa program, helping renovate and revitalize the town's commercial center. "I've always wanted to find something that fits my interest in old buildings, and through this class I've realized the importance of building the local economy. This experience helps me to put it together for my future career," Jennifer says.

Several miles to the east, Susannah Eddy, a junior in agricultural education is learning about the niche marketing potential of Iowa's local foods economy as an intern with the Henry A. Wallace Country Life Center. The forty-acre grounds contain a two-acre organic garden and one-acre organic apple orchard. When Susannah isn't teaching kids about soil quality or writing a newspaper column about vegetables, she's out in the garden, planting, harvesting, packing, or delivering vegetables for the center's community supported agriculture (CSA) program. "I'm learning a lot about niche market agriculture, and I'll have this knowledge and experience to share with students I teach in the future," she says.

In the Greene County town of Jefferson, Joseph Haley, a political science major from Burlington, assists the city manager in developing a capital improvement plan. He credits the Life in Iowa experience with affecting the way he sees Iowa and his role in the creating the future of the state.

"For me personally, this course has provided me with a framework for living well that has reinforced what I have only recently learned. Before, I had no real appreciation for my hometown or for Iowa as a whole. Gradually my thoughts changed, however. I began to realize that local issues do affect me, either directly or indirectly through the people I know and care about. And then it hit me, through my interest in local government and public administration, I could actually make a difference," Joseph says.

"Life in Iowa combines classroom theory and practice in a community," says Nancy Bevin, the program's director. "It has as its thematic center what it means for an individual to live a meaningful life and what it means to build a healthy and sustainable community."

"We're inviting broader involvement in the education of students. The problems facing Iowa now are not problems that can be reduced to what goes on in the classroom. It takes all of us working together and thinking together about the kind of future we want to create here," Nancy observes.

The program takes inspiration from environmental futurist Wes Jackson, who calls for a "homecoming major," one of going back to the community and living well in it. *In Becoming Native to this Place*, he writes, "Universities now offer only one serious major: upward mobility. Little attention is paid to educating the young to return home, or to go some other place, and dig in."

Nancy concurs. "I have found that young people who come to Iowa State today, especially if they are from rural areas, believe that if they are successful and well educated that they will move someplace else," she says. "In this program young people see opportunities in Iowa that they didn't know existed, and they are mentored by people who are themselves innovative in their communities, and envisioning a different way to live."

In contrast to most of their college classes, which require ever greater specialization, students in Life in Iowa classes consider a spectrum of interlocking topic areas covering environmental, community, political, economic, and spiritual issues. All the students are required to take the Life in Iowa class on campus before beginning their community practicum. Once out in the community, the students continue the academic portion of the course through the Internet.

Hina Patel, an ISU doctoral candidate who specializes in service learning, administers the online curriculum. "Each week the students have an assignment on a particular theme of the Living Well curriculum. It makes students more conscious of what they are learning. They are able to reflect and make connections between the curriculum and their real world experience," Hina explains.

Even though the students are scattered throughout the state to do their projects, the Internet keeps them linked to one another and to the Life in Iowa staff. As Hina reads the student's submissions, she gives each one personal attention. "Reflection contributes to higher level thinking," she asserts. "If we think of Bloom's Taxonomy, they are exploring their personal experiences with their work. I think this is a wonderful form of learning because it's challenging. It's the kind of learning that can change a person. And since we want them to become future change agents, this is a contributing factor to that form of thinking," she says.

One third of Iowa's ninety-nine counties has a Life in Iowa student during the summer of 2003. Community members are encouraged to work together to consider their future needs and then to invite a Life in Iowa student to assist with implementing the solution. The town of Larchwood in northwest Lyon County provides a good example of such community problem solving. For parents and childcare providers there, the community need was summer childcare. When Lyon County Extension education director Mary Victor learned of the concern, she gathered community members to discuss a solution. Together the group brainstormed a Kids Club with a Life in Iowa student intern as activity coordinator. Everybody pitched in. The Legion offered use of the Legion Hall, and the city provided an office. "It was one of those times when people were finding ways to solve the problems. It's that positive attitude. Everyone took responsibility instead of pointing to someone else," Mary recalls.

The Larchwood summer Kids Club runs for ten weeks. Life in Iowa intern Bill Henninger, a psychology major from Newton, works with local college student Josh Scholten in leading activities from kickball to tennis, swimming to crafts. Together they lead education clinics like Junior Ranger camps, water Olympics, and toys in space. "The kids are having so much fun, and every day they go home tired to happy parents," Mary says. The Kids Club has been so successful, surrounding communities are considering doing something similar next summer.

"The kind of work Bill is doing in Larchwood is work that has meaning," Nancy says. "It's important to the community of Larchwood, and it's an experience he'll remember all his life. Through this community-based learning experience, students are bringing to bear a new vision for Iowa. They benefit from having a chance to try their wings, try out opportunities that they didn't know about before, and being connected to people as role models who are themselves immersed in their communities."

CHANGING THE FACE OF AGRICULTURE
Denise O'Brien and the Women, Food & Agriculture Network

In mid-July 2002 a diverse group of women—farmers, urban gardeners, educators, community activists, academics, and environmentalists of all ages—joined hands and stood in a circle on a sunshiny day at central Iowa's Springbrook State Park. The nearly fifty members and friends of the Women, Food & Agriculture Network (WFAN) were celebrating the organization's fifth anniversary with a three-day summer gathering of education, fun, and strategic planning. Unremarkable? Perhaps, but this seemingly ordinary group of women is accomplishing the extraordinary task of changing the face of agriculture by acknowledging and guiding the potentially powerful role of women as rural landowners, managers, decision makers, and leaders.

It all started when Iowa organic farmer Denise O'Brien was serving as president of the National Family Farm Coalition in 1994 and met Kathy Lawrence, an activist from New York. Participating in the 1992 United Nation's Earth Summit in Rio De Janeiro, Kathy had observed that little was known about or directed toward the role of women in agriculture. To gather information and ideas on the topic worldwide, Kathy and Denise joined forces to form a Women, Food and Agriculture Working Group and sponsor a two-week workshop—"The Globalization of Agriculture"—at the 1995 United Nation's Fourth World Women's Conference in Beijing, China.

The conference provided a vital conceptual foundation for Denise, who returned to her home in Atlantic, Iowa, with the idea of finding other women who would help foster women's contribution to agriculture. Among the handful of founding members of the Women, Food & Agriculture Network was Betty Wells, an Iowa State University extension sociologist and professor of sociology. The early members were motivated "to act on our long-standing concerns about systemic rural, agricultural, and environmental problems and gender relations in these domains," Betty says. "We believe that women have valuable things to say about food, community, natural systems, and agriculture, but are too rarely heard."

The research bears her out. Women own more than 40 percent of the rentable farmland in rural America, according to a 1993 study done by the USDA Economic Research Service. Yet early WFAN research shows that the power of women to make decisions is often discounted in both interpersonal and institutional relationships. WFAN is working to change that, largely through communication and education.

In 1999, the group received a grant from the W.K. Kellogg Foundation to do three micro-enterprise workshops around Iowa on topics such as raising herbs and animals for fiber. Their purpose was to encourage women to start and run their own on-farm enterprise.

The group is also gathering information that will help direct its efforts. One third of the farms in Cass County are owned by women, and WFAN is partnering with federal and state agencies to learn about these landholders. "We wanted to know how women make decisions, where and how they get their information, and what kinds of things they'd like to do with their land," says Denise, who coordinates WFAN from the kitchen table at her family farm. "With the data gathered we hope to educate the agencies that work with women and do education for women about natural resource management so women have more information about how their farm is managed."

WFAN members share information through a quarterly newsletter, an email listserv, and retreats, including an annual Tri-State Women's Fall Harvest Gathering for Women in Sustainable Agriculture—held in cooperation with Women in Sustainable Agriculture Minnesota and the Wisconsin Women's Sustainable Farming Network. It also hosts a website at http://www.wfan.org/.

"We are developing women leaders. We have a wonderful, intergenerational group of women. Older women are mentors; younger women are emerging leaders. We have an international aspect too. We work hard to get members to international conferences. Sixty-five to seventy-five percent of the food in the world is raised by women, and we're trying to develop relationships with women farmers and landowners in other countries," explains Denise.

All of this education and information exchange seems to be having an effect. "All of a sudden last year there were programs for women in agriculture offered by organizations like Natural Resource and Conservation Service and Extension. There is an awareness of the position of women in agriculture. I'd like to think that WFAN had a major part in raising awareness and making that happen," Denise says.

In August 2000, the Iowa Commission on the Status of Women recognized Denise O'Brien's significant contribution to Iowa and Iowa women by inducting her into the Iowa Women's Hall of Fame. In nominating Denise, the late Beverly Everett described Denise as "a hands-on farmer, the woman who has one foot firmly planted on her family farm near Atlantic, and the other foot planted just as firmly on the global terra firma, calling intelligent attention to rural injustices and to the blessings of farm fresh food as food is meant to be."

The women who attended WFAN's fifth year celebration gathering recognize the group's ability to provide a safe space for women to support each other, to share knowledge, and to develop shared analyses of problems and alternative models for the future. Having grown from the initial duo and beyond the first handful of visionary women to the present membership of nearly 150 women and some men from more than twenty-five states and several countries, WFAN functions as a loosely coupled network, metaphorically clasping hands across multiple boundaries and divides—rural/urban, local/global, natural/social—to work for an equitable future.

Learning to Renew the Spirit, the Farm, and the Community

Essay by Charles Carpenter

LEARNING is a basic component of all of the ventures profiled in this book. Indeed, one could argue that learning—the acquisition of knowledge and new skills—is the most essential of the many elements that make up these efforts at rural renewal. Often the projects require human skills that have been discarded and lost. Sometimes they involve new and unique types of crops, husbandry techniques, products, or marketing strategies. And on a deeper level, these efforts always involve learning of the most profound sort—that is, psychological and spiritual growth.

My own experience in northeastern Audubon County can serve as an example. I farm 120 acres on the hillsides of Beaver Creek. My operation includes thirty beehives and a ten-acre orchard of apple, cherry, and pear trees. The apple trees are made up of noncommercial, antique varieties. These are older types of apples, once grown in this county, but not generally available any longer. They have fallen out of favor because they do not have characteristics suitable for the mass market. Our varieties include Cox's Orange Pippin, Esopus Spitzenberg (Thomas Jefferson's favorite apple), Wolf River, and Summer Rambo, among others.

The decision to grow antique apples and the process of establishing the trees and bringing the orchard into production illustrate the central importance of learning in such projects. First, my partner and I had to locate and review the available information on early apple varieties. Then we needed to find sources for the trees, along with studying the conventional information on establishing an orchard.

In 1981, we began planting trees—adding several dozen each year. We chose promising varieties, though the McIntosh was the only one we had actually sampled. For the others we relied on catalog descriptions or the suggestions of older local residents who recalled especially good apples from their childhoods.

After planting our trees, we slowly acquired the pruning techniques that are so important in maintaining the vigor of fruit trees in their first few years. After about five years, the semidwarf trees began to bear apples. As each variety began to produce, we learned firsthand the nature of the apple. The Virginia Gold (a cross between Yellow Delicious and Newton Pippin) was better than we could have imagined. On the other hand, the Sweet Winesap, described so alluringly in our catalogs, turned out to be a disappointment. After eight years of uninspired Sweet Winesaps we decided to discontinue them. But rather than cut down the trees, we took time to learn grafting techniques that would allow us to convert the trees to a different variety. By means of a grafting method called "top working," we changed the trees to an apple variety we knew would work for us—the Westfield Seek-no-Further.

Once the trees started bearing fruit, we had to develop marketing techniques to help sell these unusual apples. The public has become accustomed to the mass-marketed apple, an industrialized apple that is usually red, sweet, and crisp. Antique apples can have a wide range of surface coloring and textures (such as russetting), varying flesh colors and textures, and highly complex flavors. Selling our apples thus required us to educate our potential customers by providing information and plenty of samples.

And so it has been that our efforts with antique apple production have evolved over ten years of learning—about planting and establishing fruit trees, acquiring pruning skills, adopting disease and insect controls, selecting desirable varieties suitable in our location, applying grafting techniques, and harvesting and marketing.

But that is not all, for we have grown in deep ways as human beings as well. We have learned better observational skills. We have acquired a larger measure of patience and perseverance. Our expectations, our desires, and our hopes have been refined and reshaped. Over the years our external efforts and internal selves have been molded by the forces of nature—by the wind, the rain, and the occasional hail or wind storm, by the predations of insects and disease, the heat of summertime days, and the coolness of autumn mornings. These natural forces have shaped us as much as they have our orchard trees. This shaping has informed our intellects and honed our psyches. It has been a source of inspiration and frustration, of joy and grief. The process has created an organic bond that binds us to our farm, our landscape, and our community.

So it is for everyone engaged in rural renewal and especially for the individuals whose efforts are profiled in this book. Our efforts have not only renewed our own farms and communities, they have renewed the surrounding countryside and our spirits as well.

A native of Coon Rapids, Charles Carpenter has been a beekeeper and fruit grower there since 1979. He holds a bachelor's degree in sociology from Antioch College and a master's degree in sociology from Columbia University. His writings often appear in the Des Moines Register.

AFTERWORD

WHY would a nonprofit conservation organization like the Iowa Natural Heritage Foundation cosponsor the publication of *Renewing the Countryside?* This is our work. Together with others, we're working toward this goal of "renewing our countryside."

Iowa's landscape is severely altered and out of balance ecologically. The condition of our water and wildlife reflects how we manage our lands, and in many areas of our state both water and wildlife are in trouble. Returning life to our countryside will require people caring for the land—and one another—as stewards of Iowa.

The Iowa Natural Heritage Foundation is a nonprofit organization working exclusively in Iowa to protect Iowa's land, water and wildlife. The Foundation was created in 1979 by business and community leaders from throughout Iowa who saw the need to involve the private sector more fully in protecting Iowa's natural resources ... for those who follow.

Tens of thousands of acres of important conservation, natural, and recreation resource lands throughout Iowa have been protected through the Foundation's efforts. These lands provide important refuge for wildlife, help protect and clean our waters, encourage healthy lifestyles, and build local economies. We do this by building partnerships and educating Iowans to protect, preserve, and enhance Iowa's natural resources for future generations. In many ways our work is about "renewing the countryside."

Renewing the countryside can best be accomplished through private stewardship and public-private partnerships to protect Iowa's natural resources. We can work together to develop economically viable enterprises which encourage stewardship and provide meaningful livelihoods for our people. This will help create quality of place—so important for our citizens and visitors and the future of Iowa.

The Iowa Natural Heritage Foundation is pleased to help cosponsor this book. We feel it is important to challenge the myths that we must continue to sacrifice our natural resources in the name of economic development and that individuals cannot make a difference. Agriculture, strong businesses, and growing communities do not have to degrade our environment. In fact, they can be—must be—the tools to help restore balance and protect this special place we call Iowa.

If we do not work together to renew our countryside, we will continue to sacrifice our environment and the future of generations yet unborn. Let us choose a sustainable future. To do so will require actions now. Many of our fellow citizens depicted in this volume are helping lead the way. Let us all help them and many like them renew the Iowa countryside by supporting their efforts and encouraging others. We hope you will do your part.

Mark C. Ackelson, President
Iowa Natural Heritage Foundation

WHEN I was asked to apply for the position of director of the Leopold Center nearly four years ago, my first answer was "no." I was satisfied with my life in North Dakota, and plenty busy running my family's farm and related businesses. I thought the search committee just wanted a token farmer in the pool of candidates.

But then I came to Iowa for the interview. I met group after group of incredible people at Iowa State University, Practical Farmers of Iowa, and in the community. I was especially struck by the number of scientists (mostly young) who were passionately dedicated to a different future for agriculture. They were committed to doing research that would make farming more profitable for family farmers, less damaging to the environment, and more conducive to building strong rural communities. These were the same values I held—values that I had been struggling to implement on my own farm, and values expressed in each one of the stories in this book. I knew then, as I do now, that I didn't want to pass up the opportunity to work with a group of stellar colleagues who shared the same goals to which I was committed.

I have since traveled all over the state and spoken with hundreds of Iowans—farmers, urban and suburban dwellers, senior citizens, and students. I have met many other wonderful people who have found new ways to think about agriculture, Iowa's natural resources, and rural communities. They are living the "land ethic," as described by the Center's namesake Aldo Leopold:

"A land ethic changes the role of Homo sapiens from conqueror of the land-community to plain member and citizen of it. It implies respect for his fellow-members, and also respect for the community."

The Leopold Center is proud to be a cosponsor of this project. We think there is no better way to share Leopold's ideas than by bringing you the stories of the people and the communities presented in *Renewing the Countryside*. They are an inspiration for all of us.

Frederick Kirschenmann, Director
Leopold Center for Sustainable Agriculture

I am a fifth generation Iowan. I was born in California and my folks watched the Disneyland fireworks every night from our house. I have often wondered where I'd be now if my parents hadn't decided to come home. I'm grateful for the opportunity to grow up in Iowa with all the advantages that implies. I've traveled within the U.S. a fair bit and now that I can live anywhere, I choose to stay—because of those advantages.

Iowa, which means "beautiful land," is a changing landscape—physically, socially and economically. The Iowa Rural Development Council is a partnership of federal, state, and locally based organizations, both public and private, profit and nonprofit, and private citizens. Recognizing changes in agriculture, business climate, workforce, health, education, telecommunications, recreation, and other areas, the Council has worked for over a decade to support projects and policy that mutually benefit those areas.

"Enhancing the development potential of Iowa's rural areas and making the best use of available resources though cooperation, collaboration, and consultation" defines the mission. In short, we work at understanding our interdependence and defining ways we can help each other in a changing Iowa.

This book is a celebration of those changes. Our agriculture business subcommittee set out to tell "good news" stories about agriculture and encourage land stewardship. We are privileged to cosponsor this book because of the positive images it projects about Iowa and Iowans. Many of

the ideas shared here employ science and technology, others represent marketing genius, they embody communities working together, entrepreneurship, opportunity, a sense of place, and, in all, the work ethic and resourcefulness we prize as Iowans.

We hope *Renewing the Countryside* will inspire entrepreneurs and communities to pursue their own ideas—and we offer our resources at iowarural.org. We hope state and federal policy makers will understand the impact of these businesses and projects, and will help to craft and pass legislation to encourage continued growth in life sciences and protection of some of the richest natural resources on earth. Most of all we hope you enjoy the stories of people creating change and will do your part to create new wealth across Iowa's countryside.

We gratefully acknowledge the other cosponsors and partners who have contributed generously to *Renewing the Countryside—Iowa Edition*. For my part, I'm not watching fireworks in the night sky, but I do thank my lucky stars for the opportunity to live in the richness of the Iowa countryside, to work with the greatest and most dedicated of Iowans in the context of the Council, and to raise a sixth generation of Iowans in a place of growth and renewal.

Beth Danowsky, Executive Director
Iowa Rural Development Council

B EAUTIFUL sunrises. That is one of the things that draws me back over and over again to my home state. But recently I was back in Nevada, Iowa, for my 35th high school reunion and the 150th birthday of the town. It was a wonderful time catching up with friends and their families, some of whom had not been seen since graduation!

After a round of pictures and reminiscences, a few of us got onto my favorite subject—renewing the countryside—and what it would take to make sure that our little town had another 150 years or more of prosperous life. Everyone was clear that it was the countryside that fed the town—the bountiful crops, the trees, and yes the sunrises that brought tourists and wanderers looking for re-creation. But they were all pessimistic—some very much so—about what the future might hold in this age of cruel globalization. They were not sure what could be done to create a future for their kids that was as caring and abundant as the life we inherited from the pioneers and our parents' generation.

I so desperately wanted to have this beautiful book in my hands right then and there to show them all of the fantastic things that their neighbors from across the state were doing to help keep their towns and regions alive and well. I wanted to slowly turn the pages to show them the fantastic pictures and to read out loud the inspirational stories and long-lasting wisdom shared on these pages.

Like a good cake, however, this book had to be baked at just the right temperature for just the right length of time to be perfect. I can't wait until our next class reunion so I can give everyone in my class one of these fantastic books. It is exactly the inspiration they need to keep hope alive.

Mark Ritchie, President
Institute for Agriculture and Trade Policy

ACKNOWLEDGMENTS

The idea for collecting and telling these stories of Iowa's rural communities came to us from Mark Ritchie, president of the Institute for Agriculture and Trade Policy (IATP), and Jan Joannides, director of Renewing the Countryside (RTC). Mark came across a project in the Netherlands that told over two hundred stories about innovative individuals who are renewing the Dutch countryside. Inspired by their work, Jan and Mark pulled together a small team of people and organizations to produce a similar book for Minnesota.

Knowing there were many great stories in Iowa, the staffs of the Leopold Center for Sustainable Agriculture, the Iowa Rural Development Council, and the Iowa Natural Heritage Foundation decided to do an Iowa version of *Renewing the Countryside* in partnership with RTC and IATP. The heads of these organizatons, Fred Kirschenmann, Beth Danowsky, and Mark Ackelson, served as advisors to the project and helped raise the funds for this book. Through this project and through their everyday work, these individuals demonstrate extraordinary leadership in renewing rural Iowa.

Production of this book has been a true collaboration. Jan guided our work and coordinated the project with vision and congeniality. Jerry DeWitt crisscrossed the state, met with each of the families or businesses, and produced stunning photographs. Brett Olson provided the art direction and engaging design. The stories and essays in this book are all written by Iowans. Their work is testament to the talent, ingenuity, and generosity to be found in this state.

Among the people who made this volume possible are Anita O'Gara, vice president and director of development, and Cathy Engstrom, director of communications, at the Iowa Natural Heritage Foundation; Laura Miller, communications specialist, and April Franksain, secretary, at the Leopold Center for Sustainable Agriculture; Beth Waterhouse, writer and editor for the Minnesota volume, who helped name some of the stories in this book; and Bill Silag for his editorial counsel at a couple of key junctures as well as for writing the section introductions.

A number of organizations provided financial support, and to these we are extremely grateful. They include the Leopold Center for Sustainable Agriculture, Iowa Natural Heritage Foundation, Iowa Rural Development Council, Northwest Area Foundation, Northern Great Plains, Inc., Great Plains Institute for Sustainable Development, Humane Society of the United States, Center for Respect of Life and Environment, Practical Farmers of Iowa, and USDA—Cooperative State Research Extension and Education Service.

May readers draw as much inspiration from these pages as we did in putting them together.

Shellie Orngard
Iowa Editor

PUBLISHING PARTNERS

LEOPOLD CENTER FOR SUSTAINABLE AGRICULTURE

The Leopold Center for Sustainable Agriculture was created by the 1987 Iowa Groundwater Protection Act to identify and reduce negative environmental and social impacts of farming, develop new ways to farm profitably while conserving natural resources, and share findings with the public. The Center was named for Aldo Leopold (1887–1948), a Burlington, Iowa, native known internationally as a conservationist, ecologist, and educator. Funding for Center programs comes from state appropriations and from fees charged on nitrogen fertilizers and pesticides sold in Iowa.

Beyond its unique origin and funding arrangement, the Leopold Center is noted for its innovative research leading to positive changes in Iowa's landscape. The Center provided early and ongoing support for use of environmentally friendly hoop buildings for hog production, rotational grazing, and a late-spring soil test to reduce unnecessary applications of nitrogen fertilizer. The Center established the Bear Creek buffer project, now a National Demonstration Watershed. The Leopold Center has supported more than 250 other projects—conducted in every county in Iowa—as part of its competitive grants program. A number of the people featured in this book have directly benefited from the Center's research.

Partnering with Practical Farmers of Iowa and other organizations, the Center supports on-farm research, hosts field days, and offers workshops and conferences. Research initiatives in marketing and food systems, ecology, and policy also are taking the Center's work to many new arenas.

For more information, visit www.leopold.iastate.edu or call 515-294-3711.

IOWA NATURAL HERITAGE FOUNDATION

The Iowa Natural Heritage Foundation (INHF) builds partnerships and educates Iowans to protect, preserve, and enhance Iowa's natural resources. Founded by and for Iowans in 1979, this member-supported, nonprofit organization safeguards important natural lands and waters in Iowa, promotes improved land management, and provides leadership in developing new conservation opportunities in Iowa.

INHF is noted for permanently protecting natural lands—more than 75,000 acres to date, touching almost every Iowa county. Many of these sites were sold by willing landowners to INHF in order to create public areas—including many popular parks, wildlife areas, and recreation trails now run by state, county, or city agencies. Other INHF projects remain in private ownership but are protected by conservation easements. Though not open to the public, these sites preserve key natural resources, water quality, and wildlife habitat. INHF projects encompass wetland restoration, woodland conservation, trail development, river and stream enhancement, sustainable agriculture, water quality protection, prairie conservation, and environmental education.

INHF supported production of this book as yet another way of celebrating Iowa's best natural resources: our land and the people who live here.

For more information, visit www.inhf.org or call 515-288-1846.

IOWA RURAL DEVELOPMENT COUNCIL

The Iowa Rural Development Council (IRDC) is a collaborative partnership of individuals and organizations that have a common interest in securing a high quality of life for all Iowans, with a special focus on those who reside in rural Iowa communities. The council's work targets a wide range of issues, including affordable housing, agriculture, business development, child care, cultural and recreational opportunities, educational and social programs, healthcare, technology, telecommunications, and workforce development.

IRDC is led and supported by a diverse membership that includes over twenty federal and twenty state agencies and nearly thirty community-based organizations and private citizens. IRDC is housed at the Iowa Department of Economic Development.

The IRDC carries out its mission of improving rural development programs by identifying and addressing interdepartmental and intergovernmental barriers to rural development; improving local capacity to make informed decisions on issues of statewide interest; creating new partnerships to improve collaboration and coordination so agencies can effectively work across lines; identifying and addressing gaps in the rural development system, and encouraging experimentation with new rural development concepts.

For more information, visit www.iowarural.org or call 515-242-4875.

INSTITUTE FOR AGRICULTURE AND TRADE POLICY

Founded in 1986, the Institute for Agriculture and Trade Policy (IATP) promotes resilient communities and ecosystems through research and education, science and technology, and policy advocacy.

IATP has a long-term commitment to policy innovation and advocacy on community economic development, food, agriculture, forestry, trade, and environmental issues. IATP works with farmers, consumers, unions, environmental organizations, citizens' groups and others—both in the U.S. and around the world—to influence the direction of policy-making. IATP is working to create equitable business relationships between and among producers and companies in different countries by promoting direct sales and fair trade between producers and consumers, both within countries and across borders.

IATP's mission is to promote economic, social, and ecological sustainable development in rural communities and regions. IATP works with landowners, businesses, entrepreneurs, lenders, community leaders, and with a wide range of educational, religious, health, conservation, government, and civic organizations to foster vibrant, resilient small towns and to renew the countryside through living, working landscapes.

Much of IATP's work is designed to promote farming, forestry, ranching, and fishing methods that both protect the environment and ensure the safety of our food supply. IATP develops on-farm pollution prevention tools, promotes ecologically sound standards and certification programs, and works with producers and companies to promote food and nonfood agricultural products that are produced from sustainably grown and harvested plants and trees.

For more information, visit www.iatp.org or call 612-870-0453.

PHOTO & WRITING CREDITS

Unless otherwise noted, the beautiful photographs in this book were taken by Jerry DeWitt

Cover Photos
front cover, from left to right
    Iowa grapes
    Marcia Connell and Jan Lovell
    Iowa wind turbines
    Jason Heki
    Bee visiting wildflower
spine and inside cover (dust jacket for hardcover version)
    Girl with flowers
back cover
    Worker taking a break at Seed Savers

Front Pages Photos
p. 2   Fields in spring
p. 5   top row, left to right
    Hands of Mark Bogenrief
    Hand of Sister Betty Daugherty
    Hands of Francis Thicke
    second row, left to right
    Goat mom's hand
    Hands of Michael Nash
    third row, left to right
    Hand of Carl Kurtz
    Hand of Dan Zollars
    Hands of Bogenrief "Lady"
p. 6   Iowa landscape
p. 7   Governor Thomas Vilsack
    photo by Dyall Photography, Mt. Pleasant, Iowa
p. 10   Iowa winter landscape

Chapter One - Conservation
Introduction - written by Bill Silag
p. 12   Mississippi River in northeast Iowa
p. 13   Bee visiting wildflower
p. 13   Ancient White Park cow

Bringing Back the Tall Grass Prairie
written by Molly McGovern and Shelly Gradwell
p. 14   Carl Kurtz
p. 15   Purple cone flower

A Family's Gift to Future Generations
written by Willy Klein
p. 17   Marcia Connell, Jan Lovell, and Christopher
p. 18   Turtle

Turning Marginal Cropland into Profitable Pastures
written by Laura J. Miller
p. 21   Diane and Dave Petty and daughter Dresden
p. 22   Iowa River Ranch calves

Working Together for Healthy, Productive Woodlands
written by Larry A. Stone
p. 25   Ron Berns and sustainably harvested
    wood pile, photo by Larry A. Stone

Saving Heirloom Plant Varieties from Extinction
written by Jerry Johnson
p. 27   Worker taking a break at Seed Savers
p. 28   Heirloom apples
p. 29   Seed Savers gardens

An Iowa Farm, from the Abstract to Reality
written by Paul W. Johnson
p. 31   Iowa landscape

Chapter Two - Farming
Introduction - written by Bill Silag
p. 32   Dick Thompson's cows
p. 33   Peppers at Waterloo Farmers Market
p. 33   Boots at the Thompson farm

Sun-Ripened Hogs
written by Karol Crosbie
p. 36   Nursing piglets
p. 37   Paul Willis
p. 38   Pig huts at Willis farm

People of the Land: Establishing New Roots
written by Karol Crosbie
p. 37   Pea blossom
p. 38   Kohlrabi
p. 39   Maichoa and Blong Lee

Your Neighbor or Your Neighbor's Farm?
written by Michael Mayerfeld Bell
This story is drawn, in modified form, from *Farming for Us All: Practical Agriculture and the Cultivation of Sustainability*, by Michael Mayerfeld Bell, with Susan Jarnagin, Gregory Peter, and Donna Bauer (Pennsylvania State University Press, 2004).
p. 40   Dick Thompson

Raising Boys, Growing Vegetables, Spinning Wool
written by Denise O'Brien
p. 43   Janette Ryan-Busch and her dog
p. 45   Janette holding hand-spun yarn

Farming in Partnership with Nature
written by David L. Williams
p. 47   Iowa countryside

Chapter Three – Arts, Tourism & Culture
Introduction - written by Bill Silag
p. 48   Bogenrief stained-glass irises
p. 49   Bus at Bentonsport
p. 49   Bike at Bentonsport park

An Illuminating Business
written by Leigh Rigby-Adcock
p. 51   Bogenrief stained-glass "Lady"
p. 52   Mark and Jeanne Bogenrief
p. 52   Bogenrief lamp

Biking Where the Trains Once Ran
written by Mike Whye
p. 53   Wabash Trace bike route sign
p. 55   Dan Zollars

Van Buren Rising
written by Nate Hoogeveen
p. 56   Mill at Bonaparte
p. 58   Downtown Bonaparte

From Horseback Riding to Stargazing
written by Leigh Rigby-Adcock
p. 59   Liz Garst
p. 60   Pond at sunset
p. 61   Historic Garst home, now B&B

Building on a Community's Heritage
written by Leigh Rigby-Adcock
p. 63   Manning Hausbarn

The Value of Staying Put
written by Michael Carey

Chapter Four – Marketing
Introduction - written by Bill Silag
p. 66   Potatoes at farmers market
p. 67   Hudson Beery with Radiance Dairy
    organic milk

Marketing Vegetables Cleverley
written by Laura J. Miller
p. 68   Michelle Kirkland and Larry Cleverley
p. 69   Basket of greens

Incubating Stay-at-Home Businesses
written by Willy Klein
p. 71   Cathy Carlson
p. 72   Cathy's cookies

Milk with a Reputation
written by Shellie Orngard
p. 75   Francis Thicke and his dairy cows
p. 76   Olivia, photo by Brett Olson

Relationship Marketing in Southwest Iowa
written by Charles Carpenter
p. 77   Audubon County Family Farms apples
p. 78   David Tousain

Come Meet the People Who Grow Your Food
written by Shellie Orngard
p. 79   Downtown Farmers Market, Des Moines
p. 80   Bread basket at farmers market
p. 81   Farmer selling corn at farmers market

Marketing as Conversation
written by Mary Swalla Holmes

Chapter Five – Product Innovations
Introduction - written by Bill Silag
p. 84   Iowa wine grapes
p. 85   Tom Wahl with chestnut picker
p. 85   Wildwood SOYogurt

Iowa's Goat Cheese Pioneers
written by Karol Crosbie
p. 86   Kathy Larson, Wendy Mickle, and
         Connie Lawrance
p. 87   Northern Prairie Chevre goat

The Aesthetics of Tofu
written by Amy Hassinger
p. 89   Tom Lacina
p. 91   Soybeans

Unsour Grapes
written by Bill Witt
p. 92   Iowa grapes
p. 93   Paul Tabor
p. 94   Bottling Iowa wine

Envisioning a New Agrarian Landscape
written by Jim Rudisill
p. 95   Tom Wahl with chestnut tree
p. 97   Ripe chestnuts in husk

Iowa Ingenuity at Work
written by John Schillinger
p. 99   Tabor vineyard barn

Chapter Six - Energy
Introduction - written by Bill Silag
p. 100   Iowa wind turbines
p. 101   John Sellers
p. 101   Biodiesel delivery truck, photo by Brett Olson

Harvesting the Wind
written by Karol Crosbie
p. 102   Glenn Cannon of Waverly Light and Power
p. 103   Wind turbines in Waverly
p. 104   Waverly wind turbine

Farmers Fueling Energy Independence
Written by Leigh Rigby-Adcock
p. 105   Myron Danzer
p. 106   Soy oil
p. 107   West Central Coop biodiesel plant in Ralston

Fields of Energy
written by Jim Cooper
p. 108   John Sellers in field of switchgrass
p. 110   Iowa farm at sunset

A Better Place to Work
written by Heather Lilienthal
p. 111   Patti Cale-Finnegan
p. 112   Inside of IAMU office building
p. 113   Prairie planting outside IAMU office building

Energy Policy Transforming the Countryside
written by David Osterberg
p. 115   Iowa wind turbines

Chapter Seven – Community
Introduction - written by Bill Silag
p. 116   Sunflower Fields CSA packing line
p. 117   Birdhouses

Building a Community Food System
written by Bill Witt
p. 118   Barry Eastman and Kamyar Enshayan
p. 119   Mark Litteaur

Working Together for a Bright Future
written by Peter Nessen
p. 120   Dawn Schmidt, Park View Inn & Suites

Locally Grown Food Delivered to Your Door
written by Jerry Johnson
p. 122   Sunflower
p. 124   Michael Nash and CSA customer
p. 125   Sign at Sunflower Fields farm

Rallying around Habitat Restoration
written by Larry A. Stone
p. 126   Rich Smith, photo by Larry A. Stone

Tomatillos among the Soybeans
written by Shellie Orngard
p. 128   Eduardo Estrella at garden in Lenox
p. 129   Tomatillo

That Glorious Song of Old
written by Mary Swander

Chapter Eight - Learning
Introduction - written by Bill Silag
p. 132   Barn in Van Buren County
p. 133   Prairiewoods Center at Hiawatha
p. 133   Jason Heki's chicks

Slow Food in Iowa City
written by Karol Crosbie
p. 136   Chef Kurt Friese

Hooking People on Land Use Issues
written by Laura J. Miller
p. 137   LaVon Griffieon with youth in
         River Bend neighborhood
p. 138   LaVon and daughter Julia

Empowering Entrepreneurs
written by Shellie Orngard
p. 139   Penny Brown Huber and Tom Cory,
         former student
p. 140   Deb Shimer, Penny's former student
p. 141   Jason Heki, Penny's student

Cultivating a Spiritual Connection to the Earth
written by Jerry Johnson
p. 143   Sister Betty Daugherty
p. 144   Statue of St. Francis of Assisi

Some Things You Can't Learn in a Classroom
written by Shellie Orngard
p. 145   Joe Haley in Jefferson City
p. 146   Heidi Andeberg in Greene County

Changing the Face of Agriculture
written by Diane Ruth Phillips
p. 148   Denise O'Brien

**Learning to Renew the Spirit, the Farm, and
the Community**
written by Charles Carpenter
p. 151   Leaves

STORY CONTACTS

The following story contact information is listed in the order in which they appear in the book.

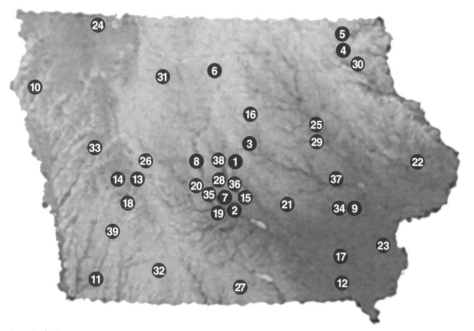

1. Carl Kurtz
   1562 Binford Avenue
   St. Anthony, IA 50239
   641-477-8364
   cpkurtz@netins.net

2. Lone Tree Point Nature Area
   Iowa Natural Heritage Foundation
   505 Fifth Avenue, Suite 444
   Des Moines, IA 50309-2321
   515-288-1846
   www.inhf.org

3. Iowa River Ranch
   Dave Petty
   32198 237th Street
   Eldora, IA 50627
   641-939-2220
   iowariverranch@netins.net

4. Prairie's Edge Sustainable Woods Cooperative
   Kevin Sand, MD, President
   1300 Big Sky Lane
   Decorah, IA 52101
   ksand@thewebunwired.com

5. Seed Savers Exchange
   3076 North Winn Road
   Decorah, IA 52101
   563-382-5990
   563-382-5872 fax
   www.seedsavers.org

6. Paul Willis and Niman Ranch
   2551 Eagle Avenue
   Thornton, IA 50479
   641-998-2683
   641-998-2683 fax
   paulw@nimanranch.com
   www.nimanranch.com

7. Maichoa and Blong Lee
   1309 Eighth Street
   Des Moines, IA 50314
   515-288-9837

8. Dick and Sharon Thompson
   2035 190th Street
   Boone, IA 50036
   515-432-1560
   dickandsharon@practicalfarmers.org

9. Janette Ryan-Busch, Fae Ridge Farm
   5140 Rapid Creek Road NE
   Iowa City, IA 52240
   319-643-5873
   Faeridge@mac.com

10. Bogenrief Studios LLC
    124 Main Street, PO Box 337
    Merrill, IA 51038
    712-938-2162; 712-938-2281
    712-938-2162 fax
    MJBogenrief@aol.com
    www.BogenriefStudios.com

11. Wabash Trace Nature Trail
    Southwest Iowa Nature Trails, Inc.
    1305 S Moreland Place
    Shenandoah, IA 51601
    www.wabashtrace.connections.net

12. Villages of Van Buren, Inc.
    PO Box 9
    Keosauqua, IA 52565
    1-800-868-7822
    319-293-7116 fax
    villages@800.tourvbc.com
    villagesofvanburen.com

13. Garst Farm Resorts
    1390 Highway 141
    Coon Rapids, IA 50058
    712-684-2964
    712-684-2887 fax
    gresort@pionet.net
    www.farmresort.com

14. Manning German Hausbarn
    320 Main Street
    Manning, IA 51455
    800-292-0252; 712-655-3131
    712-655-2941 fax
    heritage@pionet.net
    www.manningia.com

15. Cleverley Farms
    8694 Hwy 330 North
    Mingo, IA 50168
    641-363-4299
    641-363-4299 fax
    lcleverley@aol.com

16. Franklin County Cottage Industries
    Cathy's Country Cook'n
    867 130th Street
    Hampton, IA 50441
    641-579-6066
    cathyscookies@fbx.com

17. Radiance Dairy
    1745 Brookville Road
    Fairfield, IA 52556
    641-472-8554

18. Audubon County Family Farms
    2186 Goldfinch Avenue
    Audubon, IA 50025
    712-563-3044
    vcmadsen@metc.net

19. Des Moines Downtown Farmers Market
    700 Locust Street
    Des Moines, IA 50309
    515-286-4928
    515-243-6684 fax
    kfoss@downtowndsm.info
    www.downtowndsm.info

20. Northern Prairie Chevre, LLC
    Woodward, IA
    515-438-4022
    goatmom@netins.net
    www.northernprairiechevre.com

21. Wildwood Harvest Foods, Inc.
    3635 Hwy 146
    Grinnell, IA 50112
    641-236-5170
    talacina@wildwoodharvestfoods.com
    www.wildwoodharvestfoods.com

22. Tabor Home Vineyards and Winery
    3570 67th Street
    Baldwin, IA 52207
    563-673-3131
    iowawine@netins.net
    www.taborwines.com

23. Southeast Iowa Nut Growers Association
    13882 I Avenue
    Wapello, IA 52653
    319-729-5905
    redfernfarm@lisco.com
    www.redfernfarm.com

24. Spirit Lake School District
    900 20th Street
    Spirit Lake, IA 51360
    712-336-2820
    712-336-4641 fax
    tgrieves@spirit-lake.k12.ia.us
    www.spirit-lake.k12.ia.us

25. Waverly Light & Power
    PO Box 329
    Waverly, IA 50677
    319-352-6251
    www.waverlyia.com

26. West Central Cooperative
    406 First Street
    Ralston, IA 51459
    712-667-3200
    712-667-3215 fax
    myrond@westcentral.net
    www.westcentralsoy.com

27. Chariton Valley Biomass Project
    1458 160th Street
    Corydon, IA 50060
    641-872-2657
    jsellrs@grm.net
    www.cvrcd.org

28. Iowa Association of Municipal Utilities
    Patti Cale-Finnegan, Energy Services Coordinator
    1735 NE 70th Avenue
    Ankeny, IA 50021
    515-289-1999
    pcale@iamu.org
    www.iamu.org

29. UNI Local Foods Project
    Center for Energy and Environmental Education
    UNI-CEEE
    Cedar Falls, IA 50614-0293
    319-273-7575
    kamyar.enshayan@uni.edu
    www.uni.edu/ceee/foodproject

30. Sunflower Fields CSA
    776 Old Stage Road
    Postville, IA 52162
    563-864-3847
    563-864-3837
    sunspot@netins.net
    www.sunflowerfieldscsa.com

31. Park View Inn & Suites and Conference Center
    13 4th Street NE
    West Bend, IA 50597
    515-887-3611
    515-887-3614 fax
    parkview@ncn.net
    www.westbendmotel.com

32. Lenox Diversity Gardens
    AgConnect
    124 N Main Street
    Lenox, IA 50851
    641-333-4656
    agconnect@lenox.heartland.net

33. Ida County Pheasants Forever
    Rich Smith, Chapter President
    503 Morningside Street
    Ida Grove, IA 51445
    712-364-2036
    rsmith@gomaco.com

34. Devotay and Slow Food Iowa
    Chef Kurt Friese, Director
    Iowa City, IA
    www.devotay.com
    www.slowfoodiowa.com

35. 1000 Friends of Iowa
    LaVon Griffieon
    3524 Sixth Avenue
    Des Moines IA 50313
    515-288-5364
    XXVhoursaday@aol.com
    www.kfoi.org

36. Grow Your Small Market Farm
    Penny Brown Huber
    1465 NE 69th Place
    Ankeny, IA 50021
    515-289-0238
    brownpennyl@aol.com

37. Prairiewoods Franciscan Spirituality Center
    Sister Betty Daugherty
    120 E Boyson Road
    Hiawatha, IA 52233
    319-395-6700
    319-395-6703 fax
    ecospirit@prairiewoods.org
    www.prairiewoods.org

38. Life in Iowa
    Iowa State University
    101 Wallace Road Office Building
    Ames, IA 50010
    515-294-1322 or 515-294-6998
    nlbevin@iastate.edu or sorngard@iastate.edu
    www.lifelearner.iastate.edu/lifeiniowa.htm

39. Denise O'Brien and the
    Women, Food & Agriculture Network
    59624 Chicago Road
    Atlantic, IA 50022-9619
    712-243-3264
    hnob@metc.net
    www.wfan.org

Renewing The Countryside

Renewing the Countryside (RTC) began in 1998 as a joint effort of Mark Ritchie, president of the Institute for Agriculture and Trade Policy, and Jan Joannides, a rural community and sustainable development activist, after seeing a publication from the Netherlands by the same title.

They imagined a series of books, calendars, and a website that would share stories of people who are redefining what it means to live, work, and learn in rural America. While there were an abundance of stories of innovative entrepreneurs and creative community initiatives in rural areas, these stories rarely were seen in the mainstream media and almost never in the bindings of a coffee-table style book. This format gives legitimacy and validity to this new vibrancy and sustainability in the countryside.

RTC's publications expose a new group of people to a side of the rural landscape they may otherwise never hear about. They also serve as a resource guide for people to examine their own rural enterprises and help them craft more sustainable and vibrant communities.

Renewing the Countryside finds stories of rural renewal through partnerships with other organizations that not only have similar goals of strengthening rural communities and the environment, but also bring specific expertise within a region or topic area. RTC works in partnership with these organizations to champion rural communities, farmers, artists, entrepreneurs, educators, activists, and other rural heroes.

Through the generous support of many individuals and foundations, Renewing the Countryside is dedicated to sharing the strength of America's rural landscape: the people enhancing their cultural and natural resources while spurring local economic development in their communities.

www.renewingthecountryside.org

Renewing the Countryside
2105 First Avenue South
Minneapolis, Minnesota 55404 USA
1-866-378-0587
rtc@iatp.org